授業をグーンと楽しくする英語教材シリーズ **48**

フォーカス・オン・フォームを取り入れた
英文法指導ワーク
&
パフォーマンス・テスト 高校

佐藤一嘉 編著

明治図書

JN040195

まえがき

2022年度から高校1年生を対象に新学習指導要領が導入された。2024年度には，高校1年から3年まで新学習指導要領が指導目標になる。具体的な目標として，「外国語によるコミュニケーションにおける見方・考え方を働かせ，外国語による聞くこと，読むこと，話すこと，書くことの言語活動及びこれらを結び付けた統合的な言語活動を通して，情報や考えなどを的確に理解したり適切に表現したり伝え合ったりするコミュニケーションを図る資質・能力」の育成を目指すことが明記されている。特に「話すこと」については，初めて「やり取り」と「発表」の2つの領域が示され，聞くこと，読むこと，書くことと合わせて，4技能5領域を一体的に育成することが新たな目標となっている。

Savignon (1997) は，コミュニケーションの定義を "Communication is the expression, interpretation, and negotiation of meaning" (p.225) と述べている。つまり，「やり取り」とは，"negotiation of meaning" のことであり，相手との「意味の交渉」である。この点が個人の「発表」の領域と大きく異なる点である。

さらに，文部科学省は，高校の英語の授業については，基本的に英語で教えることを明記している。「英語コミュニケーション」「論理・表現」の授業で，文法をコミュニケーションの道具と捉え，4技能5領域を一体的に育成し，指導を評価に結びつけるにはどうしたらよいのだろうか？

本書は，この問いに応えるために企画された。「フォーカス・オン・フォーム」で文法をコミュニカティブに教え，「パフォーマンス・テスト」を評価に入れることで，4技能5領域を一体的に育成することができる。本書の執筆に関わった5名の高校教師（奥田，猿渡，柴田，竹内，藤本）は，名古屋外国語大学大学院 TESOL プログラムを履修して，アクション・リサーチに取り組み，「フォーカス・オン・フォーム」と「パフォーマンス・テスト」を取り入れた授業実践を継続した。その結果，生徒のモチベーションが上がり，学習効果が高まることがわかった。読者は，各教師が作成したワークシートおよび評価表から，「フォーカス・オン・フォーム」と「パフォーマンス・テスト」について学ぶことができる。全82種類のワークシートおよび評価表を収録し，中学校の復習から高校で学ぶ文法項目，さらに「論理・表現Ⅰ，Ⅱ，Ⅲ」の3年間の目標であるディスカッション，ディベートおよびエッセイ・ライティングにまで対応している。すべてのワークシートおよび評価表は，ホームページからダウンロードできるので，自由に修正して活用していただきたい。

新学習指導要領の実施に向けて，本書が新しい英語授業と評価のモデルになるものと確信している。教師が変われば，授業が変わり，生徒が変わる。

2024年4月   名古屋外国語大学教授　佐藤一嘉

Table of Contents

本書の特長と使い方

　本書では，タスクを用いた新しい英文法指導ができる「フォーカス・オン・フォーム」と「パフォーマンス・テスト」について，理論編（Part1）と実践編（Part2）にわけ，授業ですぐに役立つ形でご紹介しています！

1．本書の特長
　本書には，以下の5つの特長があります。

❶フォーカス・オン・フォームで個々の文法項目をコミュニカティブに教えることができる。

❷教科書で指導する前に英文法を効率的に教えることができるフォーカス・オン・フォームのワークシートを多数紹介。

❸まとめの活動やパフォーマンス・テスト（speaking and writing test）として使用できる review のタスクを収録。

❹各学期（1，2回実施することが望ましい）使えるパフォーマンス・テストは，事前に示すとモチベーションが上がる評価基準表（rubric）つき。

❺コミュニカティブな授業とパフォーマンス・テストの評価で，授業と評価の一体化ができる。

2．本書の使い方
　Part1では，フォーカス・オン・フォームとパフォーマンス・テストの考え方（理論）を，Part2では，タスクを用いたフォーカス・オン・フォームの英文法のアイデアやワークシートの他，パフォーマンス・テストを紹介しています。

＊【Work Sheet ページ】のデータは以下の URL からダウンロードできます。（本書に掲載されていないものも含め，1年から3年まで82種類のワークシート，藤本先生の実践報告および資料のデータもダウンロードできます。）
　URL　http://www3.nufs.ac.jp/~yoshi/index.html
　ユーザー名　formandperformance
　パスワード　sato4

❶フォーカス・オン・フォームの英文法アイデア＆ワークシート

【Task ページ】タスクの進め方，ワンポイント・アドバイス

【Work Sheet ページ】ワークシート

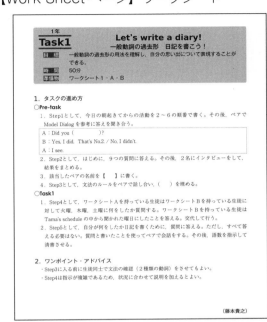

❷パフォーマンス・テスト（Review）

【Task ページ】タスクの進め方，ワンポイント・アドバイス

【Work Sheet ページ】speaking and writing test，評価表など

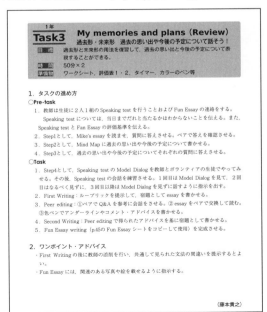

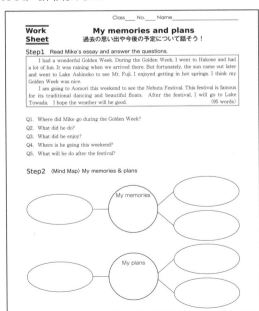

Part 1

授業を変える！
フォーカス・オン・フォーム
＆パフォーマンス・テスト
の極意

文法指導と評価の一体化について

佐藤一嘉

1. はじめに

　2022年に高校で導入された新学習指導要領のねらいはどこにあるのだろう。なぜ，「話すこと」が「やり取り」と「発表」の2つの領域にわけられたのだろう。まえがきで述べたように，コミュニケーションとは，「表現，解釈，意味の交渉」である（草野，佐藤，田中，2016）。Savignon (1997) は，さらに，コミュニケーション能力について，次のように説明している。

> Communicative competence is a *dynamic* rather than a static concept. It depends on the negotiation of meaning between two or more people who share to some degree the same symbolic system. In this sense, then, communicative competence can be said to be an *interpersonal* rather than an *intrapersonal* trait. (p.14, italics original)

　つまり，コミュニケーション能力とは，静的な概念ではなく，動的なものであり，複数の人たちの間で行われる意味の交渉によって決まる。したがって，コミュニケーション能力は個人のものというよりは，対人関係に基づくという特徴を持つ（草野，佐藤，田中，2016）。この点が，個人の「発表」の領域と大きく異なる。しかしながら，これまで中学校，高校の英語の授業では，show and tell や public speech など個人の「発表」が重視され，生徒同士の「やり取り」は軽視されてきた。コミュニケーション能力は，「暗記」ではなく，生徒同士がコミュニケーション活動を通して実際に「やり取り」をすることによってのみ，育成されることを考えると（Sato & Takahashi, 2008; Savignon, 1972, 1997），「やり取り」がもっと重視されるべきである。それでは，授業で「やり取り」と「発表」をどのように指導したらいいのだろうか？

2. 「やり取り」から「発表」へ

　ここでモデルとなるのが，Willis (1996) が提唱している Task-Based Language Teaching (TBLT) の framework である。TBLT（タスクに基づく外国語指導）とは，学習者のコミュニケーション能力の伸長を目的とする CLT (Communicative Language Teaching) を具体化した指導法の1つである。Brown (2007) は，次のように述べている。"One of the most prominent perspectives within the CLT framework is Task-Based Language Teaching (TBLT) ... TBLT is at the very heart of CLT" (p. 50).

Willis (1996) は，TBLT の framework を以下のように３段階で示している。

(1) Pre-task:
トピックの導入，
語彙や表現の導入（インプット），
タスクの目的とやり方の明示
(2) Task cycle:
ペアやグループでタスク活動（アウトプット），活動の内容をまとめ，クラスにレポート（発表）
(3) Language focus:
語彙や表現の練習（ドリル），
教師のフィードバック

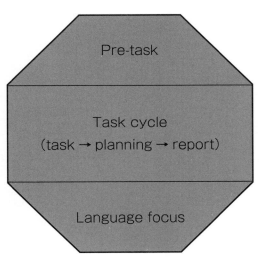

図1：TBLT framework (Willis, 1996)

　つまり，タスク（コミュニケーション活動）の後で，個人の発表へつなげればよい。例えば，"My best memory about my trip" がトピックであれば，"What is your best memory about your trip?" "When did you go there?" "What did you do?" "How many times have you been there?" などをペアで質問させ，ペアを変えて，３，４回くり返す。その後，発表の準備として（planning），絵や写真を使ってエッセイを書かせ（Fun Essay），グループで１人ずつ発表させればよい。大切な点は，ペアを変えて，生徒同士のコミュニケーション（やり取り）の時間を十分確保することである。くり返すことで，だんだん慣れ，またペアを変えることで，英語が苦手な生徒も得意な生徒に助けられて会話が続くようになる。その後，発表の準備として書かせることで，正確さにも注意をさせることができる。この場合，もし十分な時間がなければ，発表をカットすることもできる。つまり，すべてのタスクについて，発表までやる必要はない。

3. インプット重視の文法指導―「フォーカス・オン・フォーム」
　半世紀におよぶ第２言語習得研究の結果，伝統的な文法指導は効果がないことが明らかになっている。Ellis (2006) は，"a traditional approach to teaching grammar based on explicit explanations and drill-like practice is unlikely to result in the acquisition of the implicit knowledge needed for fluent and accurate communication" (p.102) と述べている。Lee & VanPattern (2003) によると，図２から明らかなように，文法説明とドリル中心の伝統的な文法指導は，十分な input がないため，学習者が新しい文法項目を自

身の第2言語のシステム（developing system）として構築することができない，と指摘している。したがって，いくら output-based instruction（ドリルやパターン・プラクティス）を与えても文法項目が定着しないわけである。

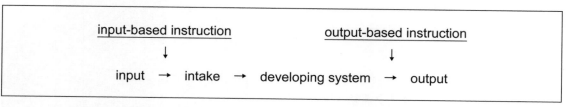

図2：第2言語習得のモデル（Lee & VanPatten, 2003を参照）

　これに対して，Ellis（2006）および Lee & VanPatten（2003）は，文法項目に焦点を当てた input-based instruction を与えることにより，学習者が文法項目に気づき（noticing），言語形式と意味を結合させ（form-meaning connections），developing system（第2言語のシステム）を構築することができると主張している。その後で学習者は，output-based instruction を通して，コミュニケーションに必要な文法項目にアクセスすることにより，アクセスのスピードが速くなり，fluency（流暢さ）や accuracy（正確さ）を伸ばすことができる，と説明している。

　要約すると，ドリルを中心とした伝統的な文法指導は意味のある input が欠如しているため，学習者が文法項目をシステムとして定着することができない。それに対して，「フォーカス・オン・フォーム」は，(1) input (2) noticing (3) output の言語習得理論の流れに基づいているため，学習者が効果的に学ぶことができる。

4. 「フォーカス・オン・フォーム」から「パフォーマンス・テスト」へ

　それでは，コミュニカティブな文法指導である「フォーカス・オン・フォーム」をどのように評価すればいいのであろう。答えは，コミュニケーション能力を測る「パフォーマンス・テスト」を実施することである。文部科学省も，2013年3月，「各中・高等学校の外国語教育における『CAN-DO リスト』の形での学習到達目標設定のための手引き」を発表し，コミュニケーション能力を測定するため，「多肢選択形式等の筆記テストのみならず，面接，エッセー，スピーチ等のパフォーマンス評価」を実施することを提唱している。さらに，2022年度から，高校においても，「指導と評価の一体化」のため観点別評価が導入され，「パフォーマンス・テスト」の実施が促された。

　Ellis（2006）は，「フォーカス・オン・フォーム」を planned focus on form（特定の文法項目にフォーカスするタスク）と incidental focus on form（特定の文法項目にフォーカスせず，学習した文法の復習のため，トピックについて自己表現をさせ，その後，教師が

common errors についてフィードバックするタスク）の２種類にわけている。そして，planned focus on form だけでなく incidental focus on form の両方のタスクを使用することを勧めている。つまり，通常は，planned focus on form で特定の文法項目を指導し，１つか２つの unit が終わったら，復習を兼ねてトピックにフォーカスした incidental focus on form を使えばよい。これによって，生徒は学習した文法項目を自己表現のためにリサイクルすることができ，言語習得を促進することができる。さらに，Lee & VanPatten (2003) は，incidental focus on form のタスクをそのまま「パフォーマンス・テスト」（スピーキング・テストやライティング）として使用することを勧めている。生徒は，授業でやった incidental focus on form がスピーキング・テストにつながることを知れば，モチベーションが上がり，熱心に取り組む（washback effect：波及効果）。これが，文部科学省が提唱する「授業と評価の一体化」である。奥田 (2014) および Fujimoto (2020) は，高校教員が同じ学年でチームを作り，「フォーカス・オン・フォーム」の教材を共有し，「パフォーマンス・テスト」に取り組んだ結果を報告している。その中で，奥田は，planned focus on form と incidental focus on form の両方のタスクを使用し，「パフォーマンス・テスト」を年５回（１，２学期：Show & Tell とペアのスピーキング・テスト，３学期：ペアのスピーキング・テスト）実施した結果，生徒のモチベーションが上がり，伝統的な文法指導よりも生徒の学習効果があったことを明らかにしている。また，この本の資料として p.６の URL に掲載されている藤本の実践報告では，英語が苦手な生徒が多数いる高校でも，「フォーカス・オン・フォーム」の活動を取り入れることによって，生徒が主体的にコミュニケーション活動に参加するようになったと報告している。

【参考文献】
Brown, H. D. (2007). *Teaching by principles: An interactive approach to language pedagogy* (3rd ed.). New York: Pearson Education, Inc.
Ellis, R. (2006). Current issues in the teaching of grammar: An SLA perspective. *TESOL Quarterly, 40*, 83-107.
Fujimoto, T. (2020). *The impact of focus-on-form instruction on Japanese senior high school students' motivation and communicative competence.* Unpublished MA thesis, Nagoya University of Foreign Studies.
Lee, J. F., & VanPatten, B. (2003). *Making communicative language teaching happen* (2nd ed.). New York: McGraw-Hill Companies, Inc.
Sato, K., & Takahashi, K. (2008). Curriculum revitalization in a Japanese high school through teacher collaboration. In D. Hayes & J. Sharkey (Eds.), *Revitalizing a program for school-age learners through curricular innovation* (pp. 205-237). Alexandria, VA: TESOL.
Savignon, S. J. (1972). *Communicative competence: An experiment in foreign language teaching.* Philadelphia, PA: Center for Curriculum Development.
Savignon, S. J. (1997). *Communicative competence: Theory and classroom practice* (2nd ed.). New York: The McGraw-Hill Companies, Inc.
Willis, J. (1996). *A framework for task-based learning.* Harlow: Longman.
奥田 (2014). パフォーマンス・テストに取り組んだ実践報告『ワーク＆評価表ですぐに使える！英語授業を変えるパフォーマンス・テスト　高校』(pp.13-28) 明治図書
草野，佐藤，田中 (2016).『コミュニケーション能力：理論と実践』（増補新版）(Savignon, 1997, Communicative competence: Theory and classroom practice の翻訳) 法政大学出版局

Part 2

フォーカス・オン・フォーム
＆パフォーマンス・テスト
アイデア

Task1

Let's write a diary!
一般動詞の過去形　日記を書こう！

目　標	一般動詞の過去形の用法を理解し，自分の思い出について表現することができる。
時　間	50分
準備物	ワークシート1・A・B

1．タスクの進め方

○Pre-task

1．Step1として，今日の朝起きてからの活動を2～6の順番で書く。その後，ペアでModel Dialog を参考に答えを聞き合う。

> A：Did you （　　　　　　）?
> B：Yes, I did. That's No.2. / No, I didn't.
> A：I see.

2．Step2として，はじめに，9つの質問に答える。その後，2名にインタビューをして，結果をまとめる。

3．該当したペアの名前を【　　】に書く。

4．Step3として，文法のルールをペアで話し合い，（　　）を埋める。

○Task1

1．Step4として，ワークシートAを持っている生徒はワークシートBを持っている生徒に対して火曜，木曜，土曜に何をしたか質問する。ワークシートBを持っている生徒はTama's schedule の中から聞かれた曜日にしたことを答える。交代して行う。

2．Step5として，自分が何をしたか日記を書くために，質問に答える。ただし，すべて答える必要はない。質問と書いたことを使ってペアで会話をする。その後，語数を指示して清書させる。

2．ワンポイント・アドバイス

・Step3に入る前に生徒同士で文法の確認（2種類の動詞）をさせてもよい。

・Step4は指示が複雑であるため，状況に合わせて説明を加えるとよい。

（藤本貴之）

Work Sheet1

Let's write a diary!
日記を書こう！

Step1   What did you do this morning?

Choose 5 things that you did this morning in order.

I got up.	(1)	I <ruby>combed<rt>くしでとく</rt></ruby> my hair.	( )
I <ruby>shaved<rt>ひげをそる</rt></ruby> my face.	( )	I took a shower.	( )
I said, "Good morning."	( )	I brushed my teeth.	( )
I went to the toilet.	( )	I had breakfast.	( )
I watched news on TV.	( )	I washed my face.	( )
I left the house.	(7)		

★ Let's check the answers.

〈Model Dialog〉

A : Did you (　　　　　)?

B : Yes, I did. That's No.2. / No, I didn't.

A : I see.

Step2   Please ask your friends!

Questions \ Name	You		
Did you shave your face?	Yes・No	Yes・No	Yes・No
Did you say, "Good morning"?	Yes・No	Yes・No	Yes・No
Did you go to the toilet?	Yes・No	Yes・No	Yes・No
Did you watch news on TV?	Yes・No	Yes・No	Yes・No
Did you comb your hair?	Yes・No	Yes・No	Yes・No
Did you take a shower?	Yes・No	Yes・No	Yes・No
Did you brush your teeth?	Yes・No	Yes・No	Yes・No
Did you have breakfast?	Yes・No	Yes・No	Yes・No
Did you wash your face?	Yes・No	Yes・No	Yes・No

★ Please write your friends' name!

【 】 combed her/his hair.	【 】 shaved her/his face.
【 】 took a shower.	【 】 said, "Good morning."
【 】 brushed her/his teeth.	【 】 went to the toilet.
【 】 had breakfast.	【 】 watched news on TV.
【 】 washed her/his face.	

誰も Yes がいない場合
は No one と書こう！

★ Let's check the answers.

〈Model Dialog〉

A：Who (combed her/his hair)?

B：(Answer).

Step3　Grammar Point

　これまでに使った英文を見直して，自分で考えて（　　　）を埋めなさい。

★過去を表現する時は動詞に（　　　　）をつけるか（　　　　　　）を用いる。

★疑問文では（　　　　　　）を文の先頭につけ，動詞は（　　　　　　）を用いる。

Work SheetA

Step4 What did Tama do last ...?

Ex) What did Tama do last Friday? He played a video game last Friday.

Tuesday _____

Thursday _____

Saturday _____

〈Pochi's schedule〉

Monday	Tuesday	Wednesday	Thursday	Friday	Saturday	Sunday
went shopping	went to the library	watched a Japanese drama	had a club activity	played a video game	studied with his friends	was sick in bed

Step5 Let's write a diary!

(1) What did you do yesterday? 【 went shopping / studied（科目）/ had club activities 】

_____

(2) What did you have for breakfast, lunch, and dinner? 【 I had 〜 for breakfast. 】

_____

(3) What did you watch on TV? 【 I watched 〜 on TV. 】

_____

(4) What did you play?

_____

(5) What subject did you study?

_____

(6) When did you wake up?

_____

(7) How long did you sleep last night?

_____

(8) Where did you go?

_____

(9) What did you buy?

_____

Work SheetB

Step4　What did Pochi do last …?

Ex）　What did Pochi do last Friday? He played a video game last Friday.

Monday

Wednesday

Sunday

〈Tama's schedule〉

Monday	Tuesday	Wednesday	Thursday	Friday	Saturday	Sunday
was sick in bed	went to the library	watched a Japanese drama	studied with his friends	played a video game	had a club activity	went shopping

Step5　Let's write a diary!

(1)　What did you do yesterday? 【 went shopping / studied（科目）/ had club activities 】

(2)　What did you have for breakfast, lunch, and dinner? 【 I had 〜 for breakfast. 】

(3)　What did you watch on TV? 【 I watched 〜 on TV. 】

(4)　What did you play?

(5)　What subject did you study?

(6)　When did you wake up?

(7)　How long did you sleep last night?

(8)　Where did you go?

(9)　What did you buy?

Task2 My future job（Review）
一般動詞　未来の自分の仕事について紹介しよう！

目　標	様々な一般動詞を使いながら未来の自分の仕事について，essay を書いたり，３分間英語で会話のやり取りを継続できるようになる。
時　間	50分×2
準備物	ワークシート１・Ａ・Ｂ，評価表１・２，タイマー

1．タスクの進め方

○Pre-task［The 1st Lesson］

1．教師は生徒に２人１組の Speaking test を行うことおよび Essay Writing の連絡をする。

2．Step1として，フライトアテンダントが自分の仕事についてインタビューを受けるという設定でリスニング活動を行う。教師が Script を読み，生徒はそれを聞いて＿＿＿に聞き取った英語を記入する。

3．Step2として，JOB Interview を行う。生徒はペアになり information gap 活動を行う。仕事についてお互いにインタビューをする。ワークシートＡを持っている生徒はユーチューバーに，ワークシートＢを持っている生徒はインタビュアーになる。その後交代して，ワークシートＢを持っている生徒がエンジニア，ワークシートＡを持っている生徒がインタビュアーになる。

4．Step3として，ブレインストーミングを行う。未来の自分の仕事についてできるだけ思いつくことを挙げる。その後クラスで共有する。ワークシートにある質問に対して簡単に答えを書いた後，ペアで会話をする。

○Task［The 2nd Lesson］

1．Step4として，First Writing を行う。未来の自分の仕事について書く。英語のエッセイライティングやパラグラフライティングの書き方に気をつけながら書く。

2．書いた essay を生徒同士で交換して読み，コメントや質問などを書き加える。内容について３つのマークを用いてコメントをする。

　a．「いいな」と思った箇所に下線を引き，☆を書く。

　b．「もっと知りたい！」と思った箇所に下線を引き，more と書く。

　c．「ここは意味がよくわからない」と思った箇所に下線を引き，？を書く。

3．Step5として，Peer editing のコメントや質問を基に内容を編集，改善，付け加えをし，語数を増やして Second Writing をする。

4．Step6として，書いた essay を基に，ペアで３分間会話をする。パートナーを代え，全４回スピーキング活動を行う。１回目は書いたものを見ながら，２回目は時々見ながら，

3回目はできるだけ見ないで，4回目は全く見ないで会話をする。会話をする際，アイコンタクトを忘れず，Communication Strategies（会話方略）を使うことをその都度伝える。
　　毎回の会話が終わった後1分程度で相手が言ったことをワークシートに記入する。話す活動が中心なので，メモ書き程度でよい。活動中は会話に集中し，書くことはさせない。
　5．Step6のスピーキング活動について振り返り，自己評価をする。

2．ワンポイント・アドバイス

　・生徒のレベルにより，ライティングの語数，スピーキング活動の継続時間や使わせる会話
　　方略を調整する。

（猿渡由果）

Work Sheet1

My future job
未来の自分の仕事について紹介しよう！

Step1　Listen to the interview about a job carefully. Write the missing words on the blanks.

〈Script〉

A : What do you do?

B : I am a _____.

A : What exactly do you do in your work?

B : I am responsible for the _____ of the passengers.
　　I try to _____ to every passenger during a flight.
　　Service includes taking care of a wide variety of needs and requests.
　　I _____ and I think it is an exciting and new
　　experience every time I fly.

A : Really? What _____ to be a flight attendant? What greatly influenced
　　you?

B : Well, it was _____ since I was a child. When I _____ with
　　my family by flight, I _____ by _____ of flight
　　attendants. That was the time when I got interested in the job as a flight attendant.

A : I see. Your dream came true. So, how do you like your job?

B : I love _____ and having new adventures.
　　I _____ for helping people and making them happy.

A : This is going to be the last question. What do you think is important to continue your
　　career?

B : This is a career where my _____. In order to give great
　　customer service, it is important to _____.
　　I would love to travel, experience new things, and I would like to do something that
　　makes me happy.

A : Thank you very much for the interview.

B : Thank you.

Work SheetA

Step2   JOB Interview

Part1 : YOU ARE [a YouTuber].

You are a YouTuber. You will get an interview from your partner at first. Here is your information.

JOB	A YouTuber
Duties : What do I do?	I create and upload videos on the YouTube online video sharing service.
Reasons why I became a YouTuber	①I don't have to be a famous TV anchor. Ordinary people like you and me can start it. I don't need a degree or anything. I just need some talent and luck. ②About one-third of the total population uses YouTube. I can have a great influence on a lot of people. If you put content out there, you'll attract people, and over time, you'll get hundreds, maybe thousands of followers. That is great!
Like JOB?	Yes. It is really a tough job because it takes a lot of time to make one video, but every time I get a great response from my followers, I feel it is worth doing.
What is important?	①You should have the techniques of video editing. ②You also need to be good at scheduling and planning. To success on YouTube, you need to put out content regularly. Once per week, twice a week, once per month. It doesn't matter. However, adding content at a steady pace is important.

Part2 : YOU ARE [an Interviewer].

You are an Interviewer. You will interview an engineer. You take notes of the interview below.

JOB	Q1. What do you do?
Duties	Q2. What exactly do you do in your work?
Reasons why s/he became an engineer	Q3. What made you decide to be an engineer? Why did you want to become an engineer?
Like JOB?	Q4. Do you like your job? Why? Why not?
What is important?	Q5. What do you think is important to be an engineer?

Work SheetB

Step2　JOB Interview

Part1：YOU ARE | an Interviewer |.

　You are an Interviewer. You will interview a YouTuber at first.　You take notes of the interview below.

JOB	Q1.　What do you do?
Duties	Q2.　What exactly do you do in your work?
Reasons why s/he became a YouTuber	Q3.　What made you decide to be a YouTuber? 　　Why did you want to become a YouTuber?
Like JOB?	Q4.　Do you like your job? Why? Why not?
What is important?	Q5.　What do you think is important to be a YouTuber?

Part2：YOU ARE | an Engineer |.

　You are an engineer. You will receive an interview from your partner next. Here is your information.

JOB	An engineer
Duties : What do I do?	I design or build machines, engines, or electrical equipment.
Reasons why I became an engineer	①Because I've always loved Math and Physics. I can use math, science and the knowledge in order to create something new every day. ②Engineering degrees are highly respected and engineers are needed all over the world. I can work wherever I want.
Like JOB?	Yes, very much. I want to come home at the end of my day and feel like I have made a difference. Being an engineer is an amazing feeling, simply because I get the joys of making and designing things that have never been before and helping people all over the world.
What is important?	You need to be a continuous learner, because we are in a time of rapid social and technological changes.

Step3 〈Brainstorming〉 What do you want to be in the future?

Brainstorm about your future job as much as possible.

What job? Duties? Why? Place? Daily schedule?

Payment? Any difficulty? What should you do in order to be …?

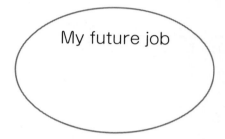

(1) What do you want to be in the future?

_____

(2) Why do you want to be …? What greatly influenced you?

_____

(3) What exactly will you do or do you want to do as a …?

_____

(4) What is your priority at work?

_____

(5) What do you think is important to be a …?

_____

(6) What should you do to make your dream come true?

_____

Step4 〈Fun Essay〉 First Writing: My future job (Write at least 80 words!)

_____

_____

_____

_____

_____

_____

_____

_____

_____

_____

Count the words you wrote : (   ) words

★ New vocabulary 調べた単語を書いておこう！

★ Peer editing（仲間同士で編集！）Questions and Comments (English or Japanese)

Editor 1　Name（   ）

(   )

Editor 2　Name（   ）

(   )

Editor 3　Name（   ）

(   )

| good | Please underline the part you think 'good' and draw ' ☆ '.
（よいと思うところに下線を引いて，星マークを書く）

| more | Please underline the part you think 'I want to know more' and write 'more'.
（もっと詳しく知りたいと思うところに下線を引いて，more と書く）

| ? | Please underline the part you think 'I don't understand well' and write '?'.
（よく意味がわからないところに下線を引いて，？を書く）

Step5 〈Fun Essay〉 Second Writing: My future job 〈Write at least 100 words!〉

_____
_____
_____
_____
_____
_____
_____
_____
_____
_____
_____
_____
_____
_____
_____
_____
_____
_____
_____
_____

Count the words you wrote : (   ) words

〈Checklist〉

☐	Is your essay interesting, informative, and easy to understand?
☐	No grammatical and spelling mistakes?
☐	Are there 3 paragraphs?
☐	Is there a topic sentence in each paragraph?
☐	Do all the supporting sentences in each paragraph support a topic sentence?
☐	Do supporting sentences give detailed information?
☐	Did you indent?
☐	Are there more than ⎡100⎤ words?

〈Example〉

My future job

    <u>I would like to be a flight attendant in the future.</u> It has been my dream since I was a child. When I traveled to Canada with my family at the age of 10 by flight, I got attracted by hospitality and smile of flight attendants. That was the time when I got interested in the job as a flight attendant. [What you want to be in the future and what greatly influenced you]

    <u>I have many things I would like to do when I become a flight attendant.</u> I love interacting with new people and having new adventures. Flight attendants are responsible for the safety and comfort of the passengers. I try to offer good service to make every passenger feel comfortable by communicating with smile. I'd love a career where my smile and hospitality matter most. I think traveling around the world is exciting. I would like to see many beautiful places, too. I think it will be an exciting and new experience every time I fly. [What exactly you will do / you want to do as a flight attendant]

    <u>In order to give great service to customers, it is important to make myself be happy and healthy.</u> I would like to do something that makes me happy. I will try to meet and communicate new people and do as many new things as possible to build experiences. I will try my best to make my dream come true. [What is important as a flight attendant and what you will do to make your dream come true]

パラグラフ構造：原則として，1つの主張（結論）とそれを支える根拠だけを書きます。1つのパラグラフは，そのパラグラフの主張を要約したTS（トピックセンテンス Topic Sentence），TSを支える根拠をまとめたSS（サポーティングセンテンス Supporting Sentence），TSを結論として別の表現で書き直したCS（コンクルーディングセンテンス Concluding Sentence）で構成します。

パラグラフ構造
TS（トピックセンテンス Topic Sentence）＝主張
SS1（サポーティングセンテンス Supporting Sentence）＝根拠①
SS2（サポーティングセンテンス Supporting Sentence）＝根拠②
CS（コンクルーディングセンテンス Concluding Sentence）＝結論（主張）

★パラグラフ（段落）を3つ作る。パラグラフを始める時はインデントする（4マス空ける）。

  パラグラフ1　[What you want to be in the future and what greatly influenced you]
        将来何になりたいか，なぜそう思うのか・思ったきっかけについて書く

  パラグラフ2　[What exactly you will do / you want to do as a …]
        その職業に就いて何をするのか，したいことについて書く

  パラグラフ3　[What is important as a … and what you will do to make your dream come true]
        その職業において大切なことは何か，自分の優先したいことは何か，夢を叶えるためにどのようなことをするのかについて書く

Step6 3 Minutes Timed-Conversation

1. Partner's name（   ）

2. Partner's name（   ）

3. Partner's name（   ）

4. Partner's name（   ）

Class____ No.____ Name_____

3 Minutes Timed-Conversation

Topic：   Date：

                                        Partner's name：

【(Self) - Evaluation（自己）評価】

(1)　Communication Strategies（会話方略）

　Please check（✔）: the Communication Strategies you used:

☐　How are you doing?　Terrific / Good / Not bad …
☐　Nice talking with you!　You, too!
☐　Me, too! / Really?　I don't.　　肯定文で（同意する・同意しない）
☐　Me, neither. / Really?　I do.　否定文で（同意する・同意しない）
☐　Repeating　（相手の言ったキーワードをくり返す）（１）
☐　Oh, really?　Oh, yeah?　I see.　そうなの？へえ〜
　　　　　　　　　　　　　　　　　　（相手の言ったことに興味を示す）（１）
☐　Sounds 〜.　〜そうだね。（１）
☐　Uh-huh.　Mm-hmm.　うん，うん。（あいづち）（１）
☐　Pardon me?　もう一度言ってくれる？
☐　Let me see.　えーと　（間をつなぐ）
☐　Follow-up questions.　（追加の質問をする）（５）

〈Step1 Answers〉

A：What do you do?
B：I am a <u>flight attendant</u>.
A：What exactly do you do in your work?
B：I am responsible for the <u>safety and comfort</u> of the passengers. I try to <u>offer excellent service</u> to every passenger during a flight. Service includes taking care of a wide variety of needs and requests. I <u>enjoy communicating with customers</u> and I think it is an exciting and new experience every time I fly.
A：Really? What <u>made you decide</u> to be a flight attendant? What greatly influenced you?
B：Well, it was <u>my dream</u> since I was a child. When I <u>traveled to Canada</u> with my family by flight, I <u>got attracted</u> by <u>hospitality and smile</u> of flight attendants. That was the time when I got interested in the job as a flight attendant.
A：I see. Your dream came true. So, how do you like your job?
B：I love <u>interacting with new people</u> and having new adventures. I <u>have a passion</u> for helping people and making them happy.
A：This is going to be the last question. What do you think is important to continue your career?
B：This is a career where my <u>smile and hospitality matter</u>. In order to give great customer service, it is important to <u>make myself be happy and healthy</u>. I would love to travel, experience new things, and I would like to do something that makes me happy.
A：Thank you very much for the interview.
B：Thank you.

【評価表1：Speaking test】

(1) 流暢さ

評価基準	得点
・3分間止まらずに英語で会話を続けることができた。 ・あいづちをうったり，関心を表したりすることを会話の中で数回行い，しかもそれが自然にできた。	10
・途切れながらも3分間，英語で会話を続けることができた。 ・あいづちをうったり，関心を表したりすることができた。	8
・時々止まってしまった。何とか3分間会話を続けることができた。 ・あいづちをうったり，関心を表したりすることがほとんどできなかった。	5
・たくさん止まってしまい，3分間会話を続けることができなかった。 ・あいづちをうったり，関心を表したりすることができなかった。	3

(2) 正確さ

評価基準	得点
・質問，答えをほとんど言い直すことなく正しく言うことができた。	7
・質問，答えを何度か言い直すことはあったが，ほぼ正しく言うことができた。	5
・質問と答えのうち半分以上は正しく言うことができた。	3
・文法がほとんど正しく使えておらず，発話もほとんど受け答えのみだった。	1

(3) 声の大きさ，アイコンタクト

評価基準	得点
・相手に十分聞こえる大きな声ではっきりと話すことができた。 ・アイコンタクトをして相手が理解しているかどうか確認しようとしていた。	3
・声の大きさかアイコンタクトのどちらかはよかったが，もう1つが不十分だった。	2
・声の大きさとアイコンタクトの両方とも不十分だった。	1

／20

【評価表2：Fun Essay】

(1) 内容

評価基準	得点
・大変よくわかり，内容も豊かで具体的である。	5
・だいたいわかるが，情報がやや足りない。	3
・内容が単純で具体例も足りない。	1

(2) 正確さ

評価基準	得点
・文法やスペルの間違いがほとんどない。	3
・2，3か所，文法やスペルの間違いがある。	2
・文法やスペルの間違いが多い。	1

(3) 語数

評価基準	得点
・100語以上書いている。	4
・90語以上書いている。	3
・80〜89語で書いている。	2
・79語以下である。	1

(4) 構成

評価基準	得点
・※パラグラフライティングができている。	3
・パラグラフライティングの要素のどこかが足りない。	2
・パラグラフライティングが全くできていない。	1

※パラグラフライティングができているとは？
①各パラグラフに Topic Sentence がある。
② Supporting Sentences は Topic Sentence を支えている。
③3つパラグラフがあり，エッセイを構成している。
④各パラグラフはインデントしている。

/15

Task3　My memories and plans（Review）

過去形・未来形　過去の思い出や今後の予定について話そう！

目　標	過去形と未来形の用法を復習して，過去の思い出と今後の予定について表現することができる。
時　間	50分×2
準備物	ワークシート，評価表1・2，タイマー，カラーのペン等

1．タスクの進め方

○Pre-task

1．教師は生徒に2人1組の Speaking test を行うことおよび Fun Essay の連絡をする。Speaking test については，当日までだれと当たるかはわからないことを伝える。また，Speaking test と Fan Essay の評価基準を伝える。

2．Step1として，Mike's essay を読ませ，質問に答えさせる。ペアで答えを確認させる。

3．Step2として，Mind Map に過去の思い出や今後の予定について書かせる。

4．Step3として，過去の思い出や今後の予定についてそれぞれの質問に答えさせる。

○Task

1．Step4として，Speaking test の Model Dialog を教師とボランティアの生徒でやってみせる。その後，Speaking test の会話を練習させる。1回目は Model Dialog を見て，2回目はなるべく見ずに，3回目以降は Model Dialog を見ずに話すように指示を出す。

2．First Writing：ルーブリックを提示して，宿題として essay を書かせる。

3．Peer editing：①ペアで Q&A を参考に会話をさせる。② essay をペアで交換して読む。③色ペンでアンダーラインやコメント・アドバイスを書かせる。

4．Second Writing：Peer editing で得られたアドバイスを基に宿題として書かせる。

5．Fun Essay writing（p.45の Fun Essay シートをコピーして使用）を完成させる。

2．ワンポイント・アドバイス

・First Writing の後に教師の添削を行い，共通して見られた文法の間違いを提示するとよい。

・Fun Essay には，関連のある写真や絵を載せるように指示する。

（藤本貴之）

Work Sheet
My memories and plans
過去の思い出や今後の予定について話そう！

Step1　Read Mike's essay and answer the questions.

> I had a wonderful Golden Week. During the Golden Week, I went to Hakone and had a lot of fun. It was raining when we arrived there. But fortunately, the sun came out later and went to Lake Ashinoko to see Mt. Fuji. I enjoyed getting in hot springs. I think my Golden Week was nice.
>
> I am going to Aomori this weekend to see the Nebuta Festival. This festival is famous for its traditional dancing and beautiful floats.　After the festival, I will go to Lake Towada.　I hope the weather will be good.
>
> (95 words)

Q1. Where did Mike go during the Golden Week?

Q2. What did he do?

Q3. What did he enjoy?

Q4. Where is he going this weekend?

Q5. What will he do after the festival?

Step2　〈Mind Map〉 My memories & plans

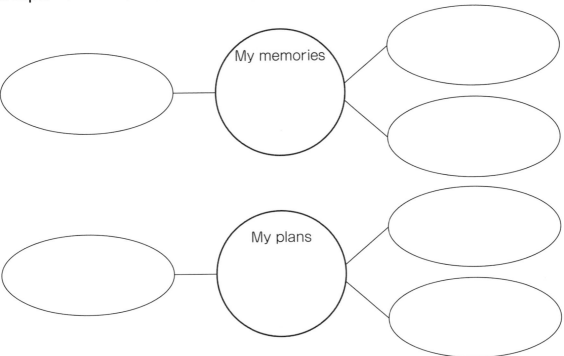

Step3 Answer the questions following the mind map!

My memories :

①What is your wonderful memory? Ex) I had a good spring vacation.

②Where did you go?

③What did you do?

④What did you enjoy?

My plans :

①What are you going to do during the summer vacation? Ex) I am going on a trip.

②Where are you going?

③Who are you going to go with?

④What will you enjoy?

Step4 Let's practice for the Speaking test!

⟨Model Dialog⟩

A : Hello, B. How are you doing?

B : Hello, A. I am (good / hungry / sleepy). How about you?

A : I am (good / hungry / sleepy).

    Let's talk about our memories.

B : Sure!

A : What is your wonderful memory?

B : I had a wonderful Golden Week.

A : ☆ Where did you go?

B : I went to Hakone.

A : ☆ What did you do?

B : I went to Lake Ashinoko to see Mt. Fuji.

A : ☆ What did you enjoy?

B : I enjoyed getting in hot springs.

A : ☆

B : How about you?

* Change roles

B : Nice talking with you.

A : You, too.

〈Communication Strategies〉（ここにあるもの以外で知っているものを使っても OK!）

Really? / Wow! / That's great! / Nice! / Sounds interesting! / Uh-huh. / I see. / Good! /
Amazing! / Me, too! / Do your best! / Good luck!

★ First Writing（homework!）　　　　　　　　　　　　（　　　　　　）words

								20
								40
								60
								80
								100

1st editor：＿＿＿＿＿＿＿	2nd editor：＿＿＿＿＿＿＿	3rd editor：＿＿＿＿＿＿＿
(Comment)	(Comment)	(Comment)

〈Peer editing〉

１．面白い，またはよい内容，自分も使ってみたい表現に下線を引き，☆をつけよう。

２．内容のわからない部分，語句に下線を引き，？をつけ，本人に確認しよう。

３．もっと聞いてみたい，詳しく知りたいところに下線を引き，[more]と書き，質問をすぐそ
　　ばに書こう。コメント欄に，友達のライティングでよかったところを書こう。

４．共感できる部分には「Me, too!」と書こう。

例１．I think ＿＿＿ ☆ is interesting for me.　　　　　　　　Thank you!!

例２．I'm sorry but I could not understand ＿＿＿?. So please tell me.

　　　　　　　　　　　　　　　　　　Ok. It means (You may use Japanese).

例３．You wrote ＿＿＿ [more]. I want to know more about it.　Ok. (You may use Japanese).

Class____ No.____ Name_____

〈Communication Strategies〉（ここにあるもの以外で知っているものを使ってもOK!）
Really? / Wow! / That's great! / Nice! / Sounds interesting! / Uh-huh. / I see. / Good! /
Amazing! / Me, too! / Do your best! / Good luck!

★ Second Writing （homework!）   (   ) words

									20
									40
									60
									80
									100

1st editor : _____	2nd editor : _____	3rd editor : _____
（Comment）	（Comment）	（Comment）

〈Peer editing〉

1．面白い，またはよい内容，自分も使ってみたい表現に下線を引き，☆をつけよう。

2．内容のわからない部分，語句に下線を引き，？をつけ，本人に確認しよう。

3．もっと聞いてみたい，詳しく知りたいところに下線を引き，more と書き，質問をすぐそ
　　ばに書こう。コメント欄に，友達のライティングでよかったところを書こう。

4．共感できる部分には「Me, too!」と書こう。

例１．I think ____ ☆ is interesting for me.　　　　　　　　　Thank you!!

例２．I'm sorry but I could not understand ____?. So please tell me.

　　　　　　　　　　　　　　　　Ok. It means (You may use Japanese).

例３．You wrote ____ more . I want to know more about it.　Ok. (You may use Japanese).

38

【評価表1：Evaluation form for Speaking test】

Categories	Criteria	Points	
(1) **Fluency & Content** なめらかさと内容	3分間なめらかに話すことができ，工夫して適切な内容を伝えようとすることができる。	10	なめらかに豊かな内容で続けられた。
		7	2，3回つかえるが適切な内容で続けられた。
		5	時々つかえ，内容が乏しかった。
		3	うまくできなかった。
		1	沈黙が長く，できなかった。
(2) **Accuracy** 正確さ	文法を間違えることなく，適切に話すことができる。	4	文法項目の間違いが1回あったが伝わった。
		3	文法項目の間違いが2，3回あったが伝わった。
		2	文法項目の間違いがところどころあったが伝わった。
		1	何を言っているのか伝わらない。
(3) **Delivery（volume & eye contact）** 態度（声の大きさとアイコンタクト）	アイコンタクトをとりながら，相手に聞こえる声で積極的に話そうとすることができる。	3	十分な声量でアイコンタクトができた。
		2	声量やアイコンタクトが十分にできなかった。
		1	声量が小さくアイコンタクトがあまりできなかった。
(4) **Communication Strategies** 会話方略	Fillers・Rejoinders を適切な場面で積極的に使うことができる。	3	3回以上適切に使った。
		2	1，2回しか使っていない。
		1	使っていない。

／20

Class＿＿＿ No.＿＿＿ Name＿＿＿＿＿＿＿＿＿＿＿＿＿＿＿＿

【評価表２：Evaluation form for Fun Essay】

Categories	Criteria	Points
(1) **Length** 長さ（語数）	・80語以上書いている。	3
	・60語以上書いている。	2
	・30語以上書いている。	1
	・29語以下である。	0
(2) **Content** 内容	・トピックについて３つ以上の側面から説明されており，単元の文法にほとんど誤りがない。	3
	・トピックについて２つの側面から説明されており，単元の文法に２，３か所誤りがある。	2
	・トピックについて説明が不十分であり，単元の文法に誤りがいくつもある。	1
	・書いていない。	0
(3) **Design** デザイン	・色の工夫や写真があり，ペンなどを効果的に使い，工夫した作品となっている。	3
	・内容が伝わるように色や写真，ペンが使われている。	2
	・白黒であり，工夫がない。	1
	・作っていない。	0

Bonus	・90語以上書いている。	1

10× 2

／20

1年

Task4
My favorite athlete（Review）
過去完了形　好きなスポーツ選手は？

目　標	過去完了形を使ってクラスメートと話したり，英文を書いたりすることができるようになる。
時　間	20分
準備物	ワークシート，評価表1・2，パワーポイント，タイマー，カラーのペン等

1. タスクの進め方

○Pre-task

1. 教師は生徒に2人1組の Speaking test を行うことおよび Fun Essay の連絡をする。Speaking test については，当日までだれと当たるかはわからないことを伝える。また，Speaking test と Fun Essay の評価基準を伝える。

2. Step1として，生徒に教師の essay を読ませ，質問に答えさせる。その後，ペアで答えの確認をさせる。

3. Step2として，好きなスポーツ選手について Mind Map を書かせる。その後，Step3で質問に答えさせる。

○Task

1. Step4として，Model Dialog を導入する。Communication Strategies の復習をする。

2. ペアを変えて，4回練習する。1回ごとに，ペアで会話が終わったら，内容について Memo に記入させる。3回目からは，Model Dialog を見ないで会話をさせる。

3. Fun Essay については，教師の essay を参考に書き始めるよう指示する。

2. ワンポイント・アドバイス

・教師の Mind Map をパワーポイントで生徒に見せることで，生徒の理解度が深まる。

・最後にパートナーと会話を練習する前に必ずもう一度評価表を見せる。

・授業終了前に必ず Speaking test に向けて練習するように生徒に伝える。

（佐藤一嘉）

My favorite athlete
好きなスポーツ選手は？

Work Sheet

Step1　Read Yoshi's essay and answer the questions.

My favorite athlete is Ichiro Suzuki. He was born in Aichi and graduated from Aikodai Meiden High School. After he had played for Orix Buffaloes for 9 years, he joined Seattle Mariners. He had been a professional baseball player for 28 years both in Japan and in USA. He had had 4367 hits in total and it is a world record. He also hit 262 in one season and it has been a world record. He retired in 2019 and became an instructor for Seattle Mariners. I admire him because he is one of the greatest Japanese baseball players in the world and is respected by many players.

(108words)

Q1.　Where was Ichiro born?

_____

Q2.　How long has he been a professional baseball player?

_____

Q3.　How many hits had he had in total?

_____

Q4.　Why does Yoshi admire Ichiro?

_____

Step2　〈Mind Map〉Choose your favorite athlete who retired.

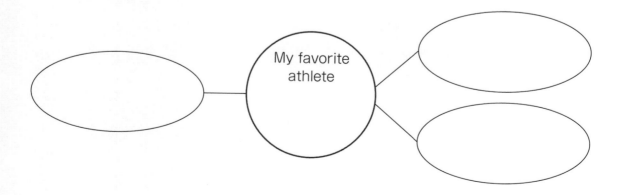

My favorite athlete

Step3 Answer the questions following the mind map!

(1) Who is your favorite athlete?

_____

(2) Why do you like him/her?

_____

(3) Please tell me more about him/her.

_____

(4) Do you have any other information?

_____

Step4 Let's practice for the Speaking test!

〈Model Dialog〉

A : Hello, B. How are you doing?

B : Hello, A. I am (good / hungry / sleepy). How about you?

A : I am (good / hungry / sleepy).

　　Let's talk about our favorite athletes.

B : Sure!

A : Who is your favorite athlete?

B : My favorite athlete is Ichiro.

A : ☆

　　Why do you like him?

B : Because he is one of the greatest Japanese baseball players in the world and is

　　respected by many players.

A : ☆

　　Please tell me more about him.

B : He had had 4367 hits in total and it is a world record.

A : ☆

　　Do you have any other information?

B : He retired in 2019 and became an instructor for Seattle Mariners.

A : ☆

B : How about you?

＊ Change roles

B : Nice talking with you.

A : You, too.

〈Communication Strategies〉（ここにあるもの以外で知っているものを使っても OK!）
Really? / Wow! / That's great! / Nice! / Sounds interesting! / Uh-huh. / I see. / Good! /
Amazing! / Me, too! / Do your best! / Good luck!

〈Memo〉

Name	①Who is your favorite athlete?	②Why do you like him/her?	③Please tell me more about him/her.	④Do you have any other information?
Ex）Yoshi	My favorite athlete is Ichiro.	One of the greatest Japanese baseball players …	He had had 4367 hits in total …	retired in 2019 …

Fun Essay:

【評価表1：Speaking test】

(1) 流暢さ

評価基準	得点
・3分間，スムーズに英語で会話を続けることができた。 ・あいづちをうったり，関心を表したりすることを会話の中で数回行い，しかもそれが自然にできた。	10
・途切れながらも3分間，英語で会話を続けることができた。 ・あいづちをうったり，関心を表したりすることができた。	8
・会話が3分間もたなかった。 ・あいづちをうったり，関心を表したりすることがほとんどできなかった。	5
・長く沈黙することがあった。あるいは途中で日本語になってしまった。 ・あいづちをうったり，関心を表したりすることができなかった。	3

(2) 正確さ

評価基準	得点
・質問，答えをほとんど言い直すことなく正しく言うことができた。	7
・質問，答えを何度か言い直すことはあったが，ほぼ正しく言うことができた。	5
・質問と答えのうち半分以上は正しく言うことができた。	3
・文法がほとんど正しく使えておらず，発話もほとんど受け答えのみだった。	1

(3) 声の大きさ，アイコンタクト

評価基準	得点
・相手に十分聞こえる大きな声ではっきりと話すことができた。 ・アイコンタクトをして相手が理解しているかどうか確認しようとしていた。	3
・声の大きさかアイコンタクトのどちらかはよかったが，もう1つが不十分だった。	2
・声の大きさとアイコンタクトの両方とも不十分だった。	1

／20

【評価表2：Fun Essay】

(1) 内容

評価基準	得点
・好きなスポーツ選手について十分書かれている。	7
・好きなスポーツ選手について書かれているが情報が物足りない。	5
・好きなスポーツ選手について少ししか書かれていない。	3
・好きなスポーツ選手についてほとんど書かれていない。	1

(2) 正確さ

評価基準	得点
・文法の誤りやスペルミスがほとんどない。	5
・文法の誤りやスペルミスが少しある。	3
・文法の誤りやスペルミスがいくつかある。	2
・文法の誤りやスペルミスがたくさんある。	1

(3) 語数

評価基準	得点
・120語以上書いている。	5
・90〜119語書いている。	3
・30〜89語書いている。	2
・29語以下である。	1

(4) デザイン

評価基準	得点
・絵が描いてあり，綺麗に仕上がっている。	3
・少し物足りないが全体的に仕上がっている。	2
・絵が描かれておらず，仕上がっていない。	1

／20

Task5

Let's learn about Malaysia!
助動詞　食文化・文化について知ろう！

目　標	助動詞の意味と使い方を理解し，タスクを通じて使えるようになる。食事のマナーや風習について知る。
時　間	20分
準備物	ワークシート1・A・B

1. タスクの進め方

○Pre-task

1. Step1として，他国の文化について，教師が例文を聞かせて，（　　）内の正しい単語を選ばせ，文が表している絵の記号を［　　］内に書かせる。

> (1) You (can / must) use your right hand.　　　　　　　　　　Picture [　　　]
>
> (2) You (must / don't have to) leave a tip on the table after eating.　Picture [　　　]
>
> (3) Muslims (don't have to / must not) eat pork.　　　　　　　Picture [　　　]
>
> ※同様に(4)～(6)も行う。

2. Step2として，ペアで答え合わせをさせる。

3. Step3として，生徒に使われている助動詞とその意味に気づかせる。

○Task

1. Step4として，ワークシートA，ワークシートBを配付する。ペアに別々のワークシートを配る。それぞれ Model Conversation を見ながらアドバイスをさせる。

2. ワンポイント・アドバイス

・国によるマナーに対しての考え方も文化の違いと言える。文化の違いから生じる価値観を理解する姿勢を大切に指導したい。

（奥田紀子）

Let's learn about Malaysia!
食文化・文化について知ろう！

Work Sheet1

Step1 Match each picture with a sentence above, and write A~F in the blank below.

マレーシアについて(1)～(6)の文を聞いて（　　）内の正しい単語に○をつけよう。また、Picture ［　　］内にあてはまる記号を書こう。

(1) You (can / must) use your right hand.　　　　　　　　Picture ［　　　］

(2) You (must / don't have to) leave a tip on the table <u>after eating</u>.　　Picture ［　　　］
<small>置く　　チップ　　　　食事の後で</small>

(3) Muslims (don't have to / must not) eat pork.　　　　Picture ［　　　］
<small>イスラム教徒</small>

(4) Hindus (don't have to / must not) eat beef.　　　　Picture ［　　　］
<small>ヒンズー教徒</small>

(5) You (may / may not) drink alcohol <u>at the age of 21</u>.　Picture ［　　　］
<small>アルコール　　21歳で</small>

(6) When you use a toothpick, you (had better / don't have to)
<small>つまようじ</small>
cover your mouth with your hands.　　　　　　　Picture ［　　　］
<small>覆う</small>

A　　　　B　　　　C　　　　D　　　　E　　　　F

Step2 Check the answer in pairs.　ペアで答えの確認をしよう。

A：This picture shows <u>（上の(1)～(6)を読み上げる）</u>. Which picture am I talking about?
<small>示す</small>

B：I think it's picture <u>（答えだと思う絵の記号）</u>. Am I right?
<small>正しい</small>

A：Yes, you are right.（No, you aren't. It's picture <u>（正しい絵の記号）</u>.）

Step3 Grammar Point　文法の確認（Noticing）

(1)～(6)で○をつけた表現がどの意味になるか、下の表に記入しよう。

やらなくてはいけないこと（強制・義務）	やってはいけないこと（禁止）	やってもよいこと（許可）	やった方がいい・やるべきこと（助言）	やらなくてもよいこと（不必要）
must	must not	may can	had better should	don't have to

★他にも知っている表現があれば、上の表に加えよう。

Work SheetA

Step4　Manners and Customs

Picture	Place	Choose the one matches the picture. 絵に合う方に○をつけなさい。
	England	You (must not / may) talk with food in the mouth. _口
	South Korea	You (should not / must) ^{茶 碗 を 持 ち 上 げ る} pick up your bowl ^{テ ー ブ ル か ら} off the table when you eat.
	France	You (must / must not) ^{音 を 立 て る} make sound when you eat soup. ^{ス ー プ}
	Japan	You (may / have to) drink alcohol outside.

★あなたは旅行に出かけます。その国のマナーや風習について，アドバイスをもらおう。

〈Model Conversation〉

A：Hi, (Toshio).　　　B：Hi, (Noriko).

A：I am planning to go to England, China, Canada, and India. Could you give me some advice?

B：Sure.　Let me see … (「え～と，」すぐに答えが出ない時に使う Conversation Strategy)

　　In England, you must not talk with food in the mouth.

A：Oh, really? / I see. / Sounds strange! / Sounds interesting!

　　When I'm in (England), I (must not) talk with food in the mouth.

B：That's right.

A：Thank you for your advice.

B：In China, you don't have to finish eating all food on your plate.

A：Oh, really? / I see. / Sounds strange! / Sounds interesting!

　　When I'm in (China), I don't have to finish eating all food on my plate.

※以下，同様に進める。

B：Have a nice trip!　　A：Thank you!

Work SheetB

Step4　Manners and Customs

Picture	Place	Choose the one matches the picture. 絵に合う方に○をつけなさい。
	England	You (must not / may) talk with food in the ^口mouth.
	China	You (don't have to / must) ^{食べ終える すべての料理を}finish eating all food on your ^皿plate.
	Canada	You (must not / must) ^{身に着ける}wear your hat at the dinner table.
	India	You (should / had better not) use your ^左left hand when you eat.

★あなたは旅行に出かけます。その国のマナーや風習について, アドバイスをもらおう。

〈Model Conversation〉

B：Hi, (Noriko).　　A：Hi, (Toshio).

B：I am planning to go to England, South Korea, France, and Japan. Could you give me some advice?

A：Sure.　Let me see … (「え～と,」すぐに答えが出ない時に使う Conversation Strategy)
In England, you must not talk with food in the mouth.

B：Oh, really? / I see. / Sounds strange! / Sounds interesting!
When I'm in (England), I (must not) talk with food in the mouth.

A：That's right.

B：Thank you for your advice.

A：In South Korea, you should not pick up your bowl off the table when you eat.

B：Oh, really? / I see. / Sounds strange! / Sounds interesting!
When I'm in (South Korea), I should not pick up my bowl off the table when I eat.

※以下, 同様に進める。

A：Have a nice trip!　　B：Thank you!

Task6　　What I regret!
should＋have＋過去分詞　こんなはずじゃなかったのに

目　標	should ＋ have ＋ 過去分詞の形式を理解し，タスクを通じて使えるようになる。
時　間	20分
準備物	ワークシート

1．タスクの進め方
○Pre-task

1．Step1として，教師が対話を聞かせ，その後の内容理解の問い（T/F）に答えさせる。

> A：Hi, Taichi.
>
> B：Hi, Noriko.
>
> A：You look very tired today. Did you sleep well last night?
>
> B：No, I didn't. I slept for only 3 hours last night. I (should / shouldn't) have slept more.
>
> A：Only 3 hours!! Why is that?
>
> B：....
>
> A：....
>
> ※ Step2の Model Conversation を参照。

2．ワークシートを配付し，Step2として，教師が再度対話を聞かせ，（　　　）内を選択させる。

3．Step3として，生徒に should ＋ have ＋ 過去分詞の形式と意味に気づかせる。

○Task

1．Step4として，状況を確認し，生徒自身が後悔したことがあるかどうか，○をつけさせる。

2．Step5として，ペアでじゃんけんをして勝った方から質問をする。自分が経験した状況を話す。終わったら，役割を交代し，会話をする。

3．Step6として，最後に自分の後悔した経験について50語程度の英語で書く。

2．ワンポイント・アドバイス

・Step1の Model Conversation は，登場人物の名前を実際の先生の名前に変えたり，サッカーの試合をその時に実際に話題になっているものに変更すると，より現実に近い場面設定にできる。

（奥田紀子）

Work Sheet

What I regret!
こんなはずじゃなかったのに

Step1　Listen to the conversation, and answer T if it is true, and F if it is false.

(1)　Noriko didn't sleep enough last night.

(2)　Noriko and Taichi played soccer yesterday.

(3)　Taichi watched the soccer game last night.

Step2　Listen to the conversation, and circle the one you hear.

〈Model Conversation〉

A : Hi, Taichi.

B : Hi, Noriko.

A : You look very tired today. Did you sleep well last night?

B : No, I didn't. I slept for only 3 hours last night. I (should / shouldn't) have slept more.

A : Only 3 hours‼ Why is that?

B : Because I was watching the soccer game on TV.

A : I see. You (should / shouldn't) have watched TV so long.

B : Well, the game was very exciting. Didn't you watch it last night?

A : No, I didn't.

B : You (should / should not) have watched it! Anyway, I will go to bed early tonight.

A : That sounds good!

Step3　Grammar Point

〈（　　　　　　）＋（　　　　　　）＋ 過去分詞〉

★「～すべきだったのに（しなかった）」という意味を表す。主語が（　　　）の時は後悔を，それ以外（You 等）の時は非難の気持ちを表すことが多い。

Step4　Which of the situation has happened to you before?

どちらかに○をつけよう。

	あなたは今まで，こんな後悔をしたことはありますか。	It has happened	It has **never** happened
1	I didn't sleep enough. I should have slept more.		
2	I didn't study hard. I should have studied harder.		
3	I ate too much. I shouldn't have eaten too much.		
4	I didn't listen to the advice. I should have taken the advice.		

Step5 Let's ask questions! Learning about friend's experience.

Step4から2つ選んで，ペアで会話をしてください。それぞれについて，2つ follow-up questions を使って，情報を聞き出してください。

1	I didn't sleep enough. I should have slept more.
	Follow-up questions: 　　How long did you sleep for?　　What were you doing? 　　What time did you wake up?　　What time did you fall asleep?
2	I didn't study hard. I should have studied harder.
	Follow-up questions: 　　Why didn't you study harder?　　Which subject didn't you study? 　　How long did you study?
3	I ate too much. I shouldn't have eaten too much.
	Follow-up questions: 　　What did you eat?　　How much did you eat?　　Why did you eat so much?
4	I didn't listen to the advice. I should have taken the advice.
	Follow-up questions: 　　What advice didn't you take?　　What was wrong? / What went wrong? 　　Who gave you the advice?

〈Model Dialog〉

A：What's wrong?

B：(I ate too much. I shouldn't have eaten too much.)

A：Oh, I'm sorry to hear that. (質問① What did you eat?)

B：Well, (あなたの答え I ate more than 10 cakes at the dessert buffet!!)

A：(相手の答えに対するコメント More than 10 cakes?! Really?) (質問② Why did you eat so much?)

B：(あなたの答え + α Because they were all so delicious, and it was my birthday!)

A：(相手へのコメント I see. Happy birthday!)

Step6 〈Writing〉 Choose one situation, and write about 50 words.

Task7
1年

My favorite country（Review）
受動態　自分の行きたい国を紹介しよう！

目　標	受動態の復習をして，自分の行きたい国について表現することができる。
時　間	50分×2
準備物	ワークシート，評価表1・2，タイマー，カラーのペン等

1. タスクの進め方

○Pre-task

1. 教師は生徒に2人1組の Speaking test を行うことおよび Fun Essay の連絡をする。Speaking test については，当日までだれと当たるかはわからないことを伝える。また，Speaking test と Fan Essay の評価基準を伝える。

2. Step1として，Quiz に答えさせ，ペアで答え合わせをさせる。

3. Step2として，自分の行きたい国について Mind Map を作成させる。

4. Step3として，5つの質問に答えさせる。

○Task

1. Step3を基に，Speaking test の会話を練習させる。1回目は Step3の質問を見て，2回目はなるべく見ずに，3回目以降は Step3の質問を見ずに話すように指示を出す。

2. Step4として，Model Essay を参考にして，First Writing を書かせる。

3. Peer editing：次の①から③を行う。

> ①ペアで2分間の会話をする。
> ②エッセイをペアで交換して読む。
> ③色ペンでアンダーラインやコメント・アドバイスを書く。

4. Second Writing：Peer editing で得られたアドバイスを基に宿題として書かせる。この時，3つ以上何を改善したのか書かせる。

5. Fun Essay writing（p.45の Fun Essay シートをコピーして使用）を完成させる。

2. ワンポイント・アドバイス

・First Writing の後に教師の添削を行い，共通して見られた文法の間違いを提示するとよい。

・Fun Essay には，関連のある写真や絵を載せるように指示する。

（藤本貴之）

Work Sheet

My favorite country
自分の行きたい国を紹介しよう！

Let's talk about our favorite country!!

Step1　Quiz "Where is this?"

(1)　This country is known for its koalas and kangaroos.　【　　　　　　　　　　】

(2)　This country is shaped like a boot.　　　　　　　　　【　　　　　　　　　　】

(3)　The Nobel Peace Prize is given in this country.　　　【　　　　　　　　　　】

(4)　John Lennon was born in this country.　　　　　　　　【　　　　　　　　　　】

(5)　The 2020 Olympic Games was held in this city.　　　　【　　　　　　　　　　】

(6)　The city is called "The Big Apple."　　　　　　　　　【　　　　　　　　　　】

(7)　The Golden Temple can be seen in this city.　　　　　【　　　　　　　　　　】

【世界地図のイラスト】

Step2　Think!　自分が選んだ国について，Mind Map を作成しよう！

Step3　Speaking test に向けて，自分の考えを書こう！

(1)　What country would you like to talk about?

(2)　What city is the capital of this country?

(3)　What language is spoken there?

(4)　What is this country known for?

(5)　What can be seen there?

Step4　Essay Writing

⟨Model Essay⟩

　　I would like to talk about my favorite country, Canada. Ottawa is the capital of this country. In this country, English and French are spoken. However, most of the people speak in English. Canada is known for its beautiful nature. For example, Niagara Falls in Ontario or Canadian Rockies in Alberta. Also, the aurora can be seen in Yellow Knife. As a souvenir, we can buy maple syrup. It is made from maple tree sap. If you are interested, why don't you visit Canada?

★ First Writing ( ) words

											10
											20
											30
											40
											50
											60
											70
											80
											90
											100
											110
											120

★コメントは下線とマークをつけた時と同じ色を使おう!!

1st editor : _____	2nd editor : _____	3rd editor : _____
(Comment)	(Comment)	(Comment)
(Advice)	(Advice)	(Advice)

〈Peer editing〉

　友達の英作文に,「もっとこうしたらいいよ」や,「もっとこんなことを書こう」という advice, そして,「もっとこんなことが知りたい」という questions を書こう!

____ ☆	面白い, またはよい内容, 自分も使ってみたい表現
____ ?	内容のわからない部分, 語句
____ more	もっと詳しく知りたいところ　質問をすぐそばに書こう。
____ me, too	共感できる部分
____ !	そうなのか, なるほどと思ったところ

Class＿＿ No.＿＿ Name＿＿＿＿＿＿＿＿＿＿＿＿

★ Second Writing （homework!）　　　　　　　　　　　（　　　　　） words

										10
										20
										30
										40
										50
										60
										70
										80
										90
										100
										110
										120

★コメントは下線とマークをつけた時と同じ色を使おう‼

1st editor : ＿＿＿＿＿＿	2nd editor : ＿＿＿＿＿＿	3rd editor : ＿＿＿＿＿＿
（Comment） （Advice）	（Comment） （Advice）	（Comment） （Advice）

★ First Writing から改善した点を３つ以上説明しよう！

【語数・内容・構成・表現について】（例：「～とアドバイスをもらい，～しました」）

Length【主体的に学習に取り組む態度】	Content【思考・判断・表現】	Total
／5	／5	／10

【評価表1 （Rubric）：Writing Assignment】

How You Are Evaluated in Fun Essay

The essay is worth a total of 10 points.

Your 'Fun Essay' is evaluated in two aspects below.

Categories	Criteria	Points
(1) **Length** 長さ（語数） 【主体的に学習に取り組む態度】	・100語以上書いてあり，First Writing からの改善が書かれている。	5
	・100語以上書いている。	3
	・80語以上書いている。	1
	・79語以下である。	0
(2) **Content** 内容 【思考・判断・表現】	・自分の興味のある国について，３つ以上の情報が具体例とともに順序だてて説明されており，文法事項が３回以上使われており，ほとんど間違いがなく，First Writing からの改善が見られる。	5
	・自分の興味のある国について，３つ以上の情報が具体例とともに順序だてて説明されており，文法事項が３回以上使われており，ほとんど間違いがない。	3
	・自分の興味のある国について，１つ以上の情報が書いてある。	1
	・書いていない。	0

文法事項【　受動態　】

〈注意点〉

①挨拶や自分の名前など，Topic に関係のない文は語数にカウントしない。

②提出に遅れた場合，【主体的に学習に取り組む態度】の点数より減点する。

③自分の言葉で会話や発表するために，また聞き手に理解してもらえるように，難しい表現を使わない。

10×2

／20

Class＿＿ No.＿＿ Name＿＿＿＿＿＿＿＿＿＿＿＿＿＿＿

【評価表２：Speaking test】

課　　題：My favorite country

実施方法：２人で２分以上のスピーキングテストを行います。ペアは当日くじで決めます。テスト中はメモを見ることはできません。テストでは時間がくるまで会話を続けてください。

観点	Categories	Criteria	Points ※a評価：8〜10点, b評価：4〜7点, C評価：3点以下
主体的に学習に取り組む態度	(1) Fluency なめらかさ	2分以上なめらかに話すことができ，工夫して適切な内容を伝えようとすることができる。	7　なめらかに豊かな内容で続けられた。 5　２，３回止まるが適切な内容で続けられた。 3　時々止まり，内容が乏しかった。 2　うまくできなかった。 1　沈黙が長く，できなかった。
	(2) Delivery (volume & eye contact) 態度（声の大きさとアイコンタクト）	アイコンタクトをとりながら，相手に聞こえる声で積極的に話そうとすることができる。	3　十分な声量でアイコンタクトができた。 2　声量やアイコンタクトが十分にできなかった。 1　声量が小さくアイコンタクトがあまりできなかった。
思考・判断・表現	(3) Content 内容	自分の意見・考えを理由，具体例や説明を加えながら，伝えることができる。	3　自分の意見・考えを理由・具体例・説明を用いながら伝えることができた。 2　自分の意見を伝えることができた。 1　自分の意見を言うことができた。 0　自分の意見を言うことができなかった。
	(4) Conversation Strategies 会話方略	Fillers, Rejoinders, Shadowing などを適切な場面で積極的に使うことができる。	3　３回以上適切に使った。 2　２回しか使っていない。 1　１回しか使っていない。 0　使っていない。
		Follow-up questions 定型文以外でその場で考えた質問をすることができる。	4　定型文以外で適切な質問が４回できた。 3　定型文以外で適切な質問が３回できた。 2　定型文以外で適切な質問が２回できた。 1　定型文以外で適切な質問が１回できた。 0　使っていない。

【主体的に学習に取り組む態度：＿＿評価】

【思考・判断・表現：＿＿評価】

／20

Task8

Jobs and dreams
不定詞の名詞的用法　将来の夢や仕事

目　標	不定詞の名詞的用法を使いながら，将来の夢や仕事について書いたり，パートナーと話したりする。
時　間	50分
準備物	ワークシート，さいころ

1. タスクの進め方

○Pre-task

1. Step1として，(1)～(8)の仕事について説明されている文をペアで読み合いながら，何の仕事か答える。その後，ペアで答えをチェックする。

2. Step2として，Step1の活動の中に含まれていたターゲットグラマー（不定詞の名詞的用法）に注目させ，フォームと意味を確認する。

○Task

1. Step3として，3人グループを作って，Board Game を行う。順にさいころをふって I want to be an/a ～ in the future. の文を使わせる。

2. Step4として，教師の Model Essay を参照して，身近な夢から大きな夢までやってみたいことや目標にしていることなどを3つ書かせる。

3. Step5として，Step4で書いた3つの夢について，パートナーとお互いにインタビューする。ペアを変えて，3，4回行う。

2. ワンポイント・アドバイス

・Step5では，Communication Strategies を使わせる。相手の言ったことに対して Oh, really?　Oh, yeah?　I see.（本当？へぇ～，なるほど）などのフレーズを使ってあいづちをうったり，相手の言ったキーワードをくり返し（shadowing），会話がスムーズになるようにする。

（猿渡由果）

Work Sheet

Jobs and dreams
将来の夢や仕事

Step1　What kind of job is this?

(1)　I like |to help| you learn new things in school.

　　　(　　　　　　　　　)

(2)　My job is |to fly| an airplane and |(to) take| passengers to a destination.

　　　(　　　　　　　　　)

(3)　I need |to take| people's orders in a restaurant and |(to) serve| them food.

　　　(　　　　　　　　　)

(4)　I love |to prepare| food for people to eat in a restaurant.

　　　(　　　　　　　　　)

(5)　My job is |to give| medical care and treatment to animals.

　　　(　　　　　　　　　)

(6)　I want |to help| people who are in trouble and need some assistance in matters relating

　　　to the law.　(　　　　　　　　　)

(7)　My job is |to work| in a bank and |(to) keep| records of money.

　　　(　　　　　　　　　)

(8)　I need |to answer| phone calls and |(to) do| office work for my boss.

　　　(　　　　　　　　　)

★ Take turns and check the answers in pairs!

A：(Read the sentences of (1)-(8).)　'What kind of job is this?' B：(Answer the name of the job.)　I think it is '_____.'

Step2　Grammar Point

Noticing（気づき）　不定詞（名詞的用法） ★[　　　]に共通している英語の形は？　（　　　　　　　　）＋（　　　　　　　） ★[　　　]に共通している英語の意味は？　（　　　　　　　　　　）

Step3　Board Game

★ I want to be a (an) ～ in the future.

| Start | → | ウエイターの
イラスト | → | 裁判官の
イラスト | → | 歌手の
イラスト |

| 画家の
イラスト | ← | 秘書の
イラスト | ← | 消防士の
イラスト | ← | Go
3 steps
forward! |

| 警察官の
イラスト | → | Miss a turn! | → | 会計士の
イラスト | → | 医者の
イラスト |

| Go
2 steps
backward! | ← | パイロットの
イラスト | ← | 美容師の
イラスト | ← | コックの
イラスト |

| 動物病院の医者の
イラスト | → | 看護師の
イラスト | → | Miss a turn! | → | サッカー選手の
イラスト |

| 宇宙飛行士の
イラスト | ← | Go back to
start! | ← | Go
3 steps
forward! | ← | 教師の
イラスト |

| 野球選手の
イラスト | → | 歯医者の
イラスト | → | Go
2 steps
backward! | → | FINISH! |

Step4　Let's write about your dreams!

★ What are your dreams?　Please list up 3 things you want to do in the future.

〈Model Essay〉

　　My dream is <u>to go</u> to Hawaii. I have two things I would like to try there. First, I would like to eat a big hamburger. Second, I would like <u>to climb</u> up Diamond Head and enjoy beautiful views of blue ocean from the top of Diamond Head.

　　My next dream is <u>to master</u> Korean language. I really <u>love to</u> watch Korean drama. Actors in Korean drama are very attractive. I also <u>like to</u> listen to K-pop music. I would like <u>to visit</u> Korea and communicate with people there using Korean.

　　My last dream is <u>to become</u> a flight attendant in the future. I've always wanted <u>to be</u> a flight attendant because I love being in the air. The more I am in the sky, the happier I am. I think it is an exciting job.

No.1

_____

_____

_____

No.2

_____

_____

_____

No.3

_____

_____

_____

Step5　Let's talk with your partner!

A : What are your dreams?

B : (Read your 3 dreams.)

Take turns. 交代する

〈Conversation Strategies〉会話方略を使って
Repeating: 相手の言ったキーワードをくり返す。
Oh, really?　Oh, yeah?　I see. 本当？へぇ〜, なるほど

Class____ No.____ Name_____

〈Answer key : input〉

(1) I like to help you learn new things in school.
(teacher   )

(2) My job is to fly an airplane and (to) take passengers to a destination.
(pilot   )

(3) I need to take people's orders in a restaurant and (to) serve them food.
(waiter   )

(4) I love to prepare food for people to eat in a restaurant.
(chief   )

(5) My job is to give medical care and treatment to animals.
(veteriarian   )

(6) I want to help people who are in trouble and need some assistance in matters relating to the law. (lawer   )

(7) My job is to work in a bank and (to) keep records of money.
(accountant   )

(8) I need to answer phone calls and (to) do office work for my boss.
(secretary   )

〈Answer key : Board Game〉

	waiter	lawer	singer
painter	secretary	firefighter	
police officer		accountant	doctor
	pilot	hair dresser	chef
veteriarian	nurse		professional soccer player
astauronaut			teacher
professional baseball player	dentist		

Task9 Wherever we are, we are always friends!!

1年

複合関係副詞　いつでも友達

目　標	複合関係副詞を用いながら２分間話せるようになる。
時　間	50分
準備物	ワークシート，タイマー

1. タスクの進め方

○Pre-task

1. Step1として，教師が３つの手紙を２回音読する。１回目は生徒にメモ等をとらせず聞かせ，どのような背景・内容なのかを考えさせる。２回目ではメモ等をとらせ，背景・内容をより深く考えさせる。その後，３つの質問をペア間で話し合わせる。

Letter1 :

　　You are leaving this town tomorrow morning. We cannot meet easily. But, remember that we are always friends. **Whenever** you miss us, you can call us and chat with us online. **Whenever** you are in trouble, we will help you. **Whenever** you come to see us, we will welcome you. We know that you will be successful **whenever** you try new things there. So, keep challenging yourself. We really wish your great fortune there.

Letter2 :

　　I am leaving this town tomorrow morning. I will definitely miss you all, but I know we are friends **wherever** we are. We don't know our future, but **wherever** we choose to live, we will meet again. Actually, if you have any chance, please visit me. I will take you **wherever** you want to go. Wish me luck.

Letter3 :

　　I am very happy to know your new life starts soon! **However** hard I tried, I couldn't achieve my goal. But, you made it! **However** challenging it was, you did not give up. **However** busy you were, you tried to manage the time. Your continuous effort reached your achievement! I respect you! Good luck with your new life!

2．Step2として，教師はStep1で読んだ手紙を再読し，生徒はあてはまる語に○をつける，もしくは空欄に適切な語句を書き取る。

3．Step3として，生徒はStep1，Step2で使用した手紙を全体的に読み，内容をより理解させる。その後，Step3で挙げられている例文を用いて複合関係副詞における意味を日本語でペアで考えさせる。

○Task

1．Step4として，今年の思い出について3つの質問に答えさせる。

2．Step5として，Model Dialog を紹介し，ペアで2分間の会話をさせる。

2．ワンポイント・アドバイス

・Step5はクラスメートに手紙を書かせるという活動に変えてもよい。その際には，Step1，Step2で用いた手紙をサンプルとするとよい。

（柴田直哉）

Work Sheet Wherever we are, we are always friends!!
いつでも友達

Step1 Listen to the teacher reading aloud three letters and try to answer the following questions.

Q1. What situation do you think these letters describe? Why do you think so?

_____

Q2. What do you think about the relationships between these three people? (Family? Classmates? Childhood Friends? International Friends?) Why do you think so?

_____

Q3. What do you think about the main messages in these three letters? Why do you think so?

_____

Step2 Listen to the teacher again and complete the letters below.

Letter1 :

You are leaving this town tomorrow morning. We cannot meet easily. But, remember that we are always friends. (When / Whenever) you miss us, you can call us and chat with us online. (When / Whenever) you are in trouble, we will help you. (When / Whenever) you come to see us, we will welcome you. We know that you will be successful (when / whenever) you try new things there. So, keep challenging yourself. We really wish your great fortune there.

Letter2 :

I am leaving this town tomorrow morning. I will definitely miss you all, but I know we are friends (   ) we are. We don't know our future, but (   ) we choose to live, we will meet again. Actually, if you have any chance, please visit me. I will take you (   ) you want to go. Wish me luck.

Letter3 :

I am very happy to know your new life starts soon! (How / However) hard I tried, I couldn't achieve my goal. But, you made it! (How / However) challenging it was, you did not give up. (   ) (   ) you were, you tried to manage the time. Your continuous effort reached your achievement! I respect you! Good luck with your new life!

Step3 Grammar Point : Read the three letters on Step2 again. After that, compare the following sentences in each section. What do you think is differences between sentences? How do these differences change the meaning? Share your ideas in Japanese.

3-1a : When you miss us, you can call us and chat with us online.

(   )

3-1b : Whenever you miss us, you can call us and chat with us online.

(   )

3-1c : Whenever you come to see us, we will welcome you.

(   )

★ When + S' + V' ～ : (   )

★ Whenever + S' + V'～ : (   ) (   )

3-2a : I will take you to the place where you want to go.

(   )

3-2b : I will take you wherever you want to go.

(   )

3-2c : I know we are friends wherever we are.

(   )

★ the place where S' + V' ～ : (   )

★ Wherever + S' + V' ～ : (   ) (   )

3-3a : How busy you were!

(   )

3-3b : However busy you were, you tried to manage the time.

(   )

★ How 形容詞／副詞 + S（主語）+ V（動詞）～! : (   )

★ However + 形容詞／副詞 + S' + V' ～ : (   )

Step4 Answer the following questions to prepare for conversation activities.

Q1. What was your good memory this year? 複合関係副詞を使って答えなさい。

_____

_____

Q2. What was your partner like? Did he or she do anything actively this year?
複合関係副詞を使って答えなさい。

_____

_____

Q3. What would you like to tell your classmates just in case that you are not in the same
classroom/school next year? 複合関係副詞を使って答えなさい。

_____

_____

Step5 Have a two-minute conversation with your partner based on the model dialog.

〈Model Dialog〉

A : Hello, how are you doing?

B : Hi, I'm (great / all right / hungry / 自分の体調や調子を話そう). You know what?
The school year ends soon. We might be in a different class/school next year.

A : Right, it was a great year. I am very happy to study with you this year.

B : Oh, thank you very much. I am also happy to study with you. We had many great
memories. For example, (Ex : However challenging English classes were), you always
(Ex : tried to share your ideas and opinions with us).

A : I really appreciate your comments. I also remember (Ex : Whenever I was in trouble),
you (Ex : helped me and dealt with problems).

B : Thank you very much! Do you have any other good memories this year?

A : Yes, (Ex : Whenever we had competitions, we did our best to win).

B : Right. (パートナーの言ったことに対してコメントをする).

A : How about you? Do you have any memories this year?

B : Let me see … (Ex : Wherever we visited for school trips, we always enjoyed travelling
around whilst making jokes).

A : (Rejoinders). (パートナーの言ったことに対してコメントをする).

B : Yes. I really hope we can be together next year. Well, (Ex : Whenever you want to
talk with me, you can visit me)!

A : You too! (Ex : Wherever we are), we are good friends.

Task10　If I had the what-if box（Review）
仮定法　もしもボックスがあったら

目　標	仮定法を使い，自分の願望について話したり，書いたりできるようになる。
時　間	50分×2
準備物	ワークシート，評価表１・２，タイマー，カラーのペン等

1．タスクの進め方
○Pre-task
1．教師は生徒に２人１組の Speaking test を行うことおよび Fun Essay の連絡をする。
　　Speaking test については，当日までだれと当たるかはわからないことを伝える。また，Speaking test と Fun Essay の評価基準を伝える。

2．Step1として，essay を読ませ，質問に答えさせる。ペアで答えを確認させた後，全体で確認する。

> 　　If I had the what-if box, I would make three wishes. First, I would say "I wish I could teleport." If I could teleport, I would not need to walk, drive a car, ride a bike, or use transportations to go anywhere. Second, I would say "I wish I were rich." If I were a rich person, I would travel around the world. Third, I would say "I wish I could speak all languages." If I could speak all languages, I would make a lot of international friends.

3．Step2として，もしもボックスがあったら何をしたいか Mind Map を書かせる。

○Task
1．Step3として，質問に答え，Task を行うための準備をする。

2．Step4として，Step3の質問の答えを基に Speaking test の練習をペアで行う。ペアを変えて何度も行う。１回ごとに，ペアで会話が終わったら，内容について表に記入させる。３回目からは，Model Dialog を見ないで会話をさせる。

2．ワンポイント・アドバイス
・Step2で Mind Map を書かせる際，机間巡視を行ったりペアで情報を共有させることで，アイデアが浮かばない生徒の補助をする。

・Speaking test のペアでの練習中は教室を回り，苦手と感じる生徒の手助けをする。

（Yoshi ゼミ）

Work Sheet

If I had the what-if box
もしもボックスがあったら

Step1　Read the passage and answer questions.

*teleport：瞬間移動する，teleportation：瞬間移動

> If I had the what-if box, I would make three wishes. First, I would say "I wish I could teleport." If I could teleport, I would not need to walk, drive a car, ride a bike, or use transportations to go anywhere. Second, I would say "I wish I were rich." If I were a rich person, I would travel around the world. Third, I would say "I wish I could speak all languages." If I could speak all languages, I would make a lot of international friends.

Q1.　What is her first wish?

_____

Q2.　If she were rich, what would she do?

_____

Q3.　If she could speak all languages, what would she do?

_____

Q4.　Do you think teleportation is useful? And why?

_____

Step2　Draw Mind Map

If you had the what-if box, what would you do? Write three wishes.

Step3 Answer some questions

Q1. If you had the what-if box, what would you say?

_____

Q2. What are two good points of your idea?

(1) _____

(2) _____

Q3. If your wish came true, what would you do?

_____

Step4 Practice for Speaking test

〈Model Dialog〉

A : Hello. How are you?

B : Hello. I'm (good / fine / sleepy / hungry). How are you?

A : I'm (good / fine / sleepy / hungry).

　　Anyway, let's talk about the what-if box.

B : Ok.

A : If you had the what-if box, what would you say?

B : If I had the what-if box, I would say "I wish I could teleport."

A : That's good! What are two good points of your idea?

B : First, we could save time if we were able to teleport.

　　Second, it would be easy for us to travel if we could teleport.

A : Sounds great.

　　If your wish came true, what would you do?

B : If my wish came true, I would travel around the world and eat delicious food.

A : That's an interesting idea.

B : How about you? If you had the what-if box, what would you say?

A : If I had the what-if box, I would say ….

　　　⋮

A : Nice talking with you.

B : Nice talking with you, too.

Class_____ No._____ Name_____

〈Memo〉

Name	What would he/she say?	Good point 1	Good point 2	What would he/she do?

Fun Essay:

_____

_____

_____

_____

_____

_____

_____

_____

(   ) words

Class_____ No._____ Name_____

【評価表1：Evaluation form for Speaking test】

Categories	Criteria	Points
(1) **Fluency** 流暢さ	・2分間スムーズに話し続けることができた。 ・Conversation Strategies を多く使うことができた。	5
	・2分間概ねスムーズに話し続けることができた。 ・Conversation Strategies を少し使うことができた。	3
	・2分間，時々沈黙があったが，最後まで話し続けることができた。 ・Conversation Strategies を多く使うことができた。	2
	・2分間話し続けることができなかった。 ・Conversation Strategies を使うことができなかった。	1
(2) **Contents** 内容	・4つの観点（Step3の答え）について明確に話すことができた。	5
	・4つの観点について概ね話すことができた。	3
	・4つの観点について内容が不明確だった。	1
(3) **Accuracy** 正確さ	・語彙の選択や文法，発音にほとんど間違いがなかった。	5
	・語彙の選択や文法，発音にいくつか間違いがあったが，言いたいことは理解できた。	3
	・語彙の選択や文法，発音に間違いが多くあった。	1
(4) **Attitude** 態度	・大きな声ではっきりと話すことができた。 ・アイコンタクトをとりながら，相手の話を聞くことができた。	5
	・相手に聞こえる程度の声で話すことができた。 ・アイコンタクトは少ししかとれなかったが相手の話を聞くことができた。	3
	・相手に聞こえにくい声で話した。 ・アイコンタクトがとれず，相手の話も聞くことができなかった。	1

／20

【評価表２：Evaluation form for Fun Essay】

Categories	Criteria	Points
(1) **Contents** 内容	・仮定法を用いた文が３文以上ある。 ・読み手に伝わりやすいように工夫されている。	7
	・仮定法を用いた文が２文ある。 ・ある程度文章がまとまっている。	5
	・仮定法を用いた文が１文ある。 ・文章はまとまっていないが伝わる。	3
	・仮定法を用いた文がない。 ・伝えたいことがわからない。	1
(2) **Accuracy** 正確さ	・文法が正しく使用されており，スペルミスもない。	5
	・文法の誤り，スペルミスが合計で３つ以内である。	3
	・文法の誤り，スペルミスが合計で４〜６つである。	2
	・文法の誤り，スペルミスが合計で７つ以上ある。	1
(3) **Length** 長さ（語数）	・50語以上書いている。	5
	・40語以上書いている。	3
	・30語以上書いている。	2
	・29語以下である。	1
(4) **Design** デザイン	・絵が描いてあり，綺麗に仕上がっている。	3
	・少し物足りないが全体的に仕上がっている。	2
	・絵が描かれておらず，仕上がっていない。	1

／20

Task11　The person who changed my life（Review）
すべての文法事項　自分に影響を与えた人を紹介しよう！

目　標	自分に影響を与えた人について順序だてて説明することができる。
時　間	50分×2
準備物	ワークシート，評価表１・２，タイマー，カラーのペン等

1．タスクの進め方

○Pre-task

1．教師は生徒に２人１組の Speaking test を行うことおよび Fun Essay の連絡をする。
　　Speaking test については，当日までにだれと当たるかはわからないことを伝える。また，
　Speaking test と Fan Essay の評価基準を伝える。

2．Step1として，Model Essay を読ませ，質問に答えさせる。ペアで答えを確認させる。

3．Step2として，自分に影響を与えた人について Mid Map を書かせる。質問に答えなが
　　ら，自分がどのように変化したのか書かせる。

○Task

1．Step3として，Speaking test の Model Dialog を教師とボランティアの生徒でやってみ
　　せる。その後，Speaking test の会話を練習させる。１回目は Model Dialog を見て，２回
　　目はなるべく見ずに，３回目以降は Model Dialog を見ずに話すように指示を出す。

2．First Writing：ルーブリックを提示して，宿題として essay を書かせる。

3．Peer editing：①ペアで Q&A を参考に話し合いをする。
　　　　　　　　　②文章をペアで交換して読む。
　　　　　　　　　③色ペンでアンダーラインやコメント・アドバイスを書く。

4．Common Errors：教師が common errors を見つけ，feedback をする。グループを作り
　　話し合いながら，何が間違いなのか考えさせる。

5．Second Writing：Peer editing で得られたアドバイスを基に宿題として書かせる。

6．Fun Essay writing（p.45の Fun Essay シートをコピーして使用）を完成させる。

2．ワンポイント・アドバイス

・自分に影響を与えた人について Mind Map を書く時に困っているようなら，Model Essay
　を Mind Map にして見せるとわかりやすい。

・Fun Essay には，関連のある写真や絵を載せるように指示する。

（藤本貴之）

Work Sheet **The person who changed my life**
自分に影響を与えた人を紹介しよう！

Step1 〈Reading〉 The person who changed my life

〈Model Essay〉

When I was a child, I liked to play sports. Especially, I played dodgeball a lot with my friends.

This is the story of when I was in the third grade in elementary school. My friend said to me, "Why don't we play basketball together?" He played for a team but I didn't know about it. He explained it. He was a member of the basketball team and they practiced twice a week. I said, "O.K." Since then, we had practiced basketball very hard. We usually had the team practice on weekends, and we played basketball after school at the park near our house. We spent so much time playing basketball. Sometimes it was so dark that we could not see the basketball. Every year, we had basketball games in my city, and we won many games. I was very excited to play basketball.

Though he and I were in the same junior high school and played basketball together, we went to different high schools. I have played basketball for many years and I have made a lot of friends. If I hadn't met him, I would not have had a lot of friends. Meeting people is very important for our lives.

(1) What kind of child was the author?

＿＿＿＿＿＿＿＿＿＿＿＿＿＿＿＿＿＿＿＿＿＿＿＿＿＿＿＿＿＿＿＿

(2) When was the author invited to the basketball?

＿＿＿＿＿＿＿＿＿＿＿＿＿＿＿＿＿＿＿＿＿＿＿＿＿＿＿＿＿＿＿＿

(3) How often did the team practice?

＿＿＿＿＿＿＿＿＿＿＿＿＿＿＿＿＿＿＿＿＿＿＿＿＿＿＿＿＿＿＿＿

(4) Why couldn't the author see the basketball when he played in the park?

＿＿＿＿＿＿＿＿＿＿＿＿＿＿＿＿＿＿＿＿＿＿＿＿＿＿＿＿＿＿＿＿

(5) Did the author play basketball with the friend in high school?

＿＿＿＿＿＿＿＿＿＿＿＿＿＿＿＿＿＿＿＿＿＿＿＿＿＿＿＿＿＿＿＿

Step2 〈Mind Map〉 Think about yourself

The person who changed
your life

(1) What kind of person were you? (Before you met the person)

_____

_____

_____

_____

(2) Who was the person who changed your life? (Write the story)

_____

_____

_____

_____

(3) How was your life changed by meeting the person?

_____

_____

_____

_____

Step3　Let's practice for the Speaking test!

〈Model Dialog〉

A : Hello, B. How are you doing?

B : Hello, A. I am (good / hungry / sleepy). How about you?

A : I am (good / hungry / sleepy).

　　Let's talk about our people who changed our lives.

B : Sure!

A : ☆ What kind of person were you?

B : I liked to play sports. I played dodgeball a lot with my friends.

A : Oh, I see.

　　☆ Who was the person who changed your life?

B : My friend I met when I was in the third grade in elementary school changed my life.

　　He was a member of the basketball team and I joined his team.

A : Really?

　　☆ How was your life changed by meeting the person?

B : I have played basketball for many years since I met him and I have made a lot of

　　friends. If I hadn't met him, I would not have had a lot of friends.

　　Meeting people is very important for our lives.

A : That's great!

B : How about you?

　　☆ Who was the person who changed your life?

＊ Change roles

B : Nice talking with you.

A : You, too.

〈Communication Strategies〉（ここにあるもの以外で知っているものを使っても OK!）

Really? / Wow! / That's great! / Nice! / Sounds interesting! / Uh-huh. / I see. / Good! /

Amazing! / Me, too! / Do your best! / Good luck!

Class____ No.____ Name_____

★ First Writing (homework!)　　　　　　　　　　（　　　　　）words

									20
									40
									60
									80
									100
									120
									140
									160
									180

★コメントは下線とマークをつけた時と同じ色を使おう‼

1st editor：_____	2nd editor：_____	3rd editor：_____
（Good Points）	（Good Points）	（Good Points）
（Advice）	（Advice）	（Advice）

〈Peer editing〉

1．面白い，またはよい内容，自分も使ってみたい表現に下線を引き，☆をつけよう。

2．内容のわからない部分，語句に下線を引き，？をつけ，本人に確認しよう。

3．もっと詳しく知りたいところに下線を引き，more と書き，質問をすぐそばに書こう。

4．共感できる部分には「Me, too!」と書こう。

5．コメント欄に，友達ライティングのよかったところとアドバイスを書こう。Second Writing につながるアドバイスをしよう‼

Common Errors (Person who changed your life)

(1) I was shy to talk to people.

_____

(2) It was the teacher I met in the third grade of junior high school that changed my life.

_____

(3) If I have not met him, I have not have practiced so hard.

_____

(4) I said OK.

_____

(5) When I was in junior high school, I want to play the piano.

_____

(6) If I didn't meet the friend, I would not have made many friends.

_____

(7) From there, we were good friends.

_____

(8) I like there songs.

_____

(9) I had not dream for my future when I was a child.

_____

(10) I enjoyed to play sports.

_____

(11) I was difficult.

_____

Common Errors (Person who changed your life)

(1) I was shy to talk to people.

I was too shy to talk to people.

---

(2) It was the teacher I met in the third grade of junior high school that changed my life.

He was the teacher I met in the third grade of junior high school, who changed my life.

---

(3) If I have not met him, I have not have practiced so hard.

If I had not met him, I would not have practiced so hard.

---

(4) I said OK.

I said, "OK."

---

(5) When I was in junior high school, I want to play the piano.

When I was in junior high school, I wanted to play the piano.

---

(6) If I didn't meet the friend, I would not have made many friends.

If I hadn't met him/her, I would not have made many friends.

---

(7) From there, we were good friends.

Since then (From then on), we have been good friends.

---

(8) I like there songs.

I like their songs.

---

(9) I had not dream for my future when I was a child.

I did not have a dream for my future when I was a child.

---

(10) I enjoyed to play sports.

I enjoyed playing sports.

---

(11) I was difficult.

It was difficult.

★ Second Writing (homework!)   (   ) words

									20
									40
									60
									80
									100
									120
									140
									160
									180

★コメントは下線とマークをつけた時と同じ色を使おう!!

1st editor : _____	2nd editor : _____	3rd editor : _____
(Good Points)	(Good Points)	(Good Points)
(Advice)	(Advice)	(Advice)

Words	Length	Content	Total
	／7	／3	／10

【評価表1（Rubric）：Writing Assignment】

How You Are Evaluated in Fun Essay

Your 'Fun Essay' is evaluated in four aspects:

① Length ② Accuracy ③ Content ④ Design

The essay is worth a total of 20 points.

Categories	Criteria	Points
(1) **Length** 長さ（語数）	・150語以上書いている。	5
	・130語以上書いている。	3
	・110語以上書いている。	2
	・109語以下である。	1
(2) **Accuracy** 正確さ	・文法の誤りやスペルミスがほとんどない。	5
	・文法の誤りやスペルミスが少しある。	3
	・文法の誤りやスペルミスがいくつかある。	2
	・文法の誤りやスペルミスがたくさんある。	1
(3) **Content** 内容	・自分が影響を受けた人との物語が豊富な情報と具体的なストーリーとともに順序だてて説明されている。	7
	・自分が影響を受けた人との物語が説明されている。	5
	・自分が影響を受けた人との物語が説明されているが箇条書きのようで単調である。	3
	・書いていない。	0
(4) **Design** デザイン	・色の工夫や写真があり，ペンなどを効果的に使い，工夫した作品となっている。	3
	・内容が伝わるように色や写真，ペンが使われている。	2
	・白黒であり，工夫がない。	1
	・作っていない。	0

／20

【評価表2：Speaking test】

課　　題：The person who changed my life

実施方法：2人で3分以上のスピーキングテストを行います。ペアは当日くじで決めます。テスト中はメモを見ることはできません。テストでは時間がくるまで会話を続けてください。

観点	Categories	Criteria	Points ※a評価：8〜10点，b評価：4〜7点，C評価：3点以下	
主体的に学習に取り組む態度	(1) **Fluency** なめらかさ	3分以上なめらかに話すことができ，工夫して適切な内容を伝えようとすることができる。	7 5 3 2 1	なめらかに豊かな内容で続けられた。 2，3回止まるが適切な内容で続けられた。 時々止まり，内容が乏しかった。 うまくできなかった。 沈黙が長く，できなかった。
	(2) **Delivery** **(volume & eye contact)** 態度（声の大きさとアイコンタクト）	アイコンタクトをとりながら，相手に聞こえる声で積極的に話そうとすることができる。	3 2 1	十分な声量でアイコンタクトができた。 声量やアイコンタクトが十分にできなかった。 声量が小さくアイコンタクトがあまりできなかった。
思考・判断・表現	(3) **Content** 内容	自分の意見・考えを理由，具体例や説明を加えながら，伝えることができる。	3 2 1 0	自分の意見・考えを理由・具体例・説明を用いながら伝えることができた。 自分の意見を伝えることができた。 自分の意見を言うことができた。 自分の意見を言うことができなかった。
	(4) **Conversation Strategies** 会話方略	Fillers, Rejoinders, Shadowing などを適切な場面で積極的に使うことができる。	3 2 1 0	3回以上適切に使った。 2回しか使っていない。 1回しか使っていない。 使っていない。
		Follow-up questions 定型文以外でその場で考えた質問をすることができる。	4 3 2 1 0	定型文以外で適切な質問が4回できた。 定型文以外で適切な質問が3回できた。 定型文以外で適切な質問が2回できた。 定型文以外で適切な質問が1回できた。 使っていない。

　　　　　　　　　　　　　　　　　　　　　　　　　　　　　　／20

Task12 **Ping pong debate**
すべての文法事項　反ばくを用いないディベートに挑戦！

目　標	Ping pong debate（反ばくを用いない）に挑戦する。
時　間	50分×2
準備物	ワークシート

1. タスクの進め方

○Pre-task

1. Step1：教師がトピック（例：TV games）を導入して，proposition（提案：School children should not use TV games.）を示す。

2. Step2：生徒をペアにして，affirmative（賛成），negative（反対）のサイドを決めさせる。それぞれのサイドについて，理由を2つずつ考えさせる。

○Task

1. Step3：Model Dialog にしたがって，お互いの理由を言わせ，相手が要約する。ペアを変えて，3，4回くり返す。要約をする際は，

> "Let me summarize what you said,"
> "You mean …,"
> "You said …,"

などを使わせる。

2. 賛成，反対のそれぞれのサイドの中で，3人グループを作る。話し合いをさせて，よい理由を2つ選ばせる。

3. 理由1，2を述べる生徒，要約をする生徒（3人目）を決めさせる。

4. Step4：Step3の Model Dialog にしたがって，3on3で Ping pong debate を教室の前でやらせる。他の生徒は，どちらのチームが勝ったのか評価をする。

2. ワンポイント・アドバイス

・宿題として，事前に賛成，反対の両方の理由を調べさせるとよい。両方のサイドの準備をさせておく。3人グループおよびサイドは，Ping pong debate の当日に決める。

・時間があれば，debate の後，Essay Writing までさせるとよい。

（佐藤一嘉）

Work Sheet   **Ping pong debate**
反ばくを用いないディベートに挑戦！

Step1 Listen to the teacher about the topic for a debate.

Step2 Choose your side (affirmative, negative) in pairs and write down two reasons.

Resolution : School children should not use TV games.

Your side (   )

Reason 1	
Reason 2	

Step3 Let's practice summarizing in pairs.

⟨Model Dialog⟩

A : How are you doing?

B : I'm Ok. How about you?

A : I'm pretty good. Let's talk about TV games. I am for TV games for two reasons.
　　First, ... Second, ... For these two reasons, I am for TV games.

B : <u>Let me summarize what you said.</u> You are for TV games for two reasons. First, ...
　　Second, ... For these two reasons, you are for TV games.

A : That's right. How about you?

B : I'm against TV games for two reasons. First, ... Second, ... For these two reasons, I
　　am against TV games.

A : Let me summarize your points ...

B : Nice talking with you.

A : You, too.

Step4 Ping pong debate（3 on 3）

Affirmative side (Pros)　　　　　　　　　　　　　　Negative side (Cons)

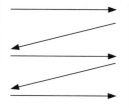

Affirmative side (Pros)	Negative side (Cons)
1. The first argument	1. Summary, the first argument
2. Summary, the second argument	2. Summary, the second argument
3. Summary of two pro arguments, conclusion	3. Summary of two pro arguments, conclusion

90

Dream jobs（Review）

現在形・過去形・未来形　高校卒業から10年後の同窓会

目　標	現在形・過去形・未来形（それぞれの進行形，完了形を含む）を適切に使って，場面に応じた会話と作文で，自分の未来について表現できるようになる。
時　間	約50分×2（2コマ）
準備物	ワークシート，評価表1・2，名刺用のカード，タイマー，カラーのペン等

1. タスクの進め方

○Pre-task

1．次のパフォーマンステストの概要を伝える。Speaking test と Essay Writing の評価基準を発表する。

2．Step1として，ALT（または生徒一人）と，Model Dialog を読み紹介する。

3．Step2として，Mind Map を作成させる。文章でなく，キーワードで記入することを確認し，思いついたことをどんどん書いていくように指導する。

4．Step3として，5つの質問に対して自分の答えを書かせる。

5．Step4として，Your Business Card（下書き）を説明する。必ず含む項目を確認し，Sample cards を見せる。実際の英語の名刺があれば，紹介する。

6．Step5として，オリジナルの質問を作成させる。質問が完成したら，それぞれに自分の答えを書かせる。

○Task

1．Step6として，Speaking test の練習をペアで行う。ペアを変えて数回行う。1回ごとに，ペアで会話が終わったら，内容について表に記入させる。3回目からは，Model Dialog を見ないで会話をさせる。その際，Step3にある質問だけでなく，Step5で作成したオリジナルの質問や会話の流れに沿った即興の質問にもチャレンジするよう促す。

2．Step7として，Essay Writing（宿題）の説明をする。思いつくままに書くのではなく，構成を考えさせる（メモを作成）。次回の授業で，2名ずつ Speaking test を受ける際，待っている生徒は Essay Writing を書き始める。評価基準を踏まえて Essay Writing と名刺を書くように指示をする。

2. ワンポイント・アドバイス

・Mind Map でペンが進まない生徒が多い場合は，Step2までやった後に，ペアを変えて，Mind Map をお互いに見せながら，3つずつ質問する時間を設ける。相手に聞かれたことから，アイデアを得て，考えを膨らませることができる。

（竹内愛子）

Work Sheet

Dream jobs
高校卒業から10年後の同窓会

Suppose you are going to see your old classmates at a reunion in ten years, 2034. You will talk about the current job, the past (experiences between now and then), and the future!

Step1　Read the model dialog and instructions in Japanese below. Then, listen to the model dialog between the ALT and the JET.

〈Model Dialog〉

場面設定：高校卒業から10年後の同窓会。会話例をどんどんアレンジして，できるだけ多くの人と話そう！

質問の役，回答の役と決めないで，自然の流れで，お互いに，今の仕事のこと，これまでのこと，これからのこと等，聞きたいことを聞く。相手が答えてくれたら，部分的にシャドーウイングしたり，リアクションしたりするのを忘れずに。これまでに習ったCommunication Strategies を使うこと。

A：Hi, (partner's name). How have you been?

B：Hi, (partner's name). Long time no see.

A：What are you doing recently?

B：Actually, I'm working for ＿＿＿＿＿ in ＿＿＿＿＿ as ＿＿＿＿＿. How about you?
　　　　　　　　　　　　　　　(company)　　(location)　　(occupation)

A：Well, I've been working for ＿＿＿＿＿ in ＿＿＿＿＿ as ＿＿＿＿＿. Please take my business card.

B：Oh, thank you. This is so cool.

A：Can I please have yours?

B：Sure. Here you are.

A：Thank you, (partner's name). Yours is so professional.
　　I'm so glad that you've made your dream come true.

B：Thank you, (partner's name).
　　It's great to see you again. And I'm happy to know you've found your dream job.

A：Please keep in touch!

B：I will.

Step2 〈Mind Map〉 Make your mind map about the topic. Expand your ideas.

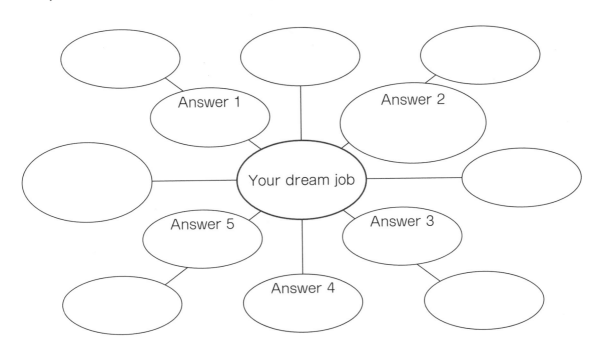

Answer 1 · Answer 2 · Answer 3 · Answer 4 · Answer 5 · Your dream job

Step3 Questions on this topic

Q1. What is your dream job? Why?

_____

Q2. Tell me about your dream job in detail. (Hint : 5W1H)

_____

Q3. How did you learn about the job?

_____

Q4. What do you have to do to make your dream come true?

_____

Q5. What do you want to do if you become a/an _____?

_____

Step4   You will make your own business card! You must include the points below.

必ず含む項目：Your name, Company name, Title（肩書き）, Slogan of the company（スローガン）, Address, Telephone number, Email address

入れてもよい項目：Degree（学位）, Qualification / License（資格／免許）, Picture, Symbol mark, etc.

★本番用の名刺カードを配付します。

【Your Business Card（下書き）】

〈Sample cards〉

【Your Business Card（本番用）】

Step5 Make the original questions you want to ask your classmates (2 WH questions + 2 Yes/No questions), then write your answer to them.

★ WH question

(1) Q : _____?

A : _____.

(2) Q : _____?

A : _____.

★ Yes/No question

(1) Q : _____?

A : _____.

(2) Q : _____?

A : _____.

Step6 Practice with your classmates. Based on Step1, 2, and 3, you will talk with your classmates. You can ask your original questions above. Also, it is good to ask incidental questions with a good flow in the conversation (会話の中で流れに沿ったその時に思いついた質問◎). Make sure to use the conversation strategies you have learned. You have three minutes in each session. Confirm both of you have chances to ask questions to each other.

〈Memo〉

Partner's Name	Dream Job	Impressive Points

Step7 Essay Writing（homework!）

Look at your mind map and review QA section again and think about the structure of your English essay. Check the rubric (Evaluation form2) before writing.

〈Structure Notes〉
・Introduction

・Body 1

・Body 2

・Conclusion

Title：_____

_____
_____
_____
_____
_____
_____
_____
_____
_____
_____
_____
_____
_____

（   ）words

※本番用の名刺カードとこの用紙を一緒に提出すること。

【評価表1：Speaking test】

観点		評価基準	得点
(1) 話し方	Attitude Delivery	・話す時は必ずアイコンタクトをして，表情豊かに，コミュニケーションを積極的にとろうという態度で話せた。	2
		・時々，相手の目を見ずに話したり，表情がなかったり，コミュニケーションを積極的にとろうという態度ではなかった。	1
		・ほとんど相手の目を見ずに話したり，表情がなかったり，消極的な態度でコミュニケーションをとっていた。	0
	Pronunciation Voice	・常に英語らしい発音で，大きな声で明瞭に話せた。	2
		・概ね英語の発音のミスなく，聞こえる声で話せた。	1
		・カタカナ発音，日本語の使用，聞き取りにくいところのある話し方だった。	0
(2) 流暢さ	Skills	・様々な Fillers や Comments，聞き返しの表現を使うことができた（5種類以上）。	2
		・Fillers や Comments，聞き返しの表現を少し使うことができた（3，4種類）。	1
		・Fillers や Comments，聞き返しの表現をほとんど使うことができなかった（0〜2種類）。	0
	Fluency	・沈黙なく，3分間，流暢に会話を続けることができた。	2
		・5秒くらいの不自然な間は1，2回あったが，ある程度会話を続けることができた。	1
		・5秒くらいの不自然な間が何度もあったり，長い沈黙があったり，会話をあまり続けられなかった（会話をせず，終了のベルが鳴るのを待った）。	0
(3) 内容	Contents	・すべての質問や回答が，テーマ（話の流れ）に適切だった。	2
		・質問や回答が，時々，テーマ（話の流れ）からそれることがあった。	1
		・質問や回答が，よくテーマ（話の流れ）からそれた。	0
(4) 正確さ	Accuracy	・質問も回答も，概ね正確に伝えることができた。	2
		・（文法・語彙に）時々，間違いがあったが，伝えることができた。	1
		・（文法・語彙に）よく間違いがあり，正確に伝えることができなかった。	0

／12

【評価表2：Essay Writing】

	観点	評価基準	得点
(1) 量	**Length**	・100語以上書いている。	4
		・81〜99語書いている。	3
		・61〜80語書いている。	2
		・60語以下である。	1
(2) 構成	**Structure**	・適切な4段落構成で，段落同士のつながりもよい。ディスコースマーカーを適切に3回以上使用している。	4
		・4段落構成で書いているが，段落同士のつながりがよくない。または，ディスコースマーカーを3回以上使用しているが，誤った使用が含まれる。	3
		・4段落構成で書いていない。または，ディスコースマーカーの使用が2回。	2
		・4段落構成で書いていない。または，ディスコースマーカーの使用が1回以下。	1
(3) 内容	**Contents**	・オリジナリティのある内容で，具体的に，読者にわかりやすく書いている。現在・過去・未来すべてに言及している。	4
		・具体的に書いているが，オリジナリティがやや弱い。現在・過去・未来すべてに言及している。	3
		・オリジナリティのある内容だが，具体性に欠ける。現在・過去・未来のうち2つしか言及していない。または，同じことをくり返し書いている。	2
		・オリジナリティも，具体性も欠ける。または，現在・過去・未来のうち1つしか言及していない。	1
(4) 正確さ	**Accuracy**	・適切な文法，語彙，つづり，符号を用いて書いている。誤りなし。	4
		・誤り1，2つ。	3
		・誤り3，4つ。	2
		・誤り5つ以上。	1
(5) 名刺	**Design**	・条件にある情報（必ず含む項目）をすべて含み，魅力的なオリジナリティのあるデザインで，カラーで作成している。	4
		・条件にある情報（必ず含む項目）をすべて含み，魅力的なデザインであるが，オリジナリティに欠ける。または，鉛筆書きか一色のペンのみで作成している。	3
		・必ず含む項目を1，2つ含んでいない。	2
		・必ず含む項目を3つ以上含んでいない。	1

／20

Task14 My endeavor and accomplishment（Review）
すべての文法事項　自分が達成したことや努力したこと

目　標	自分が達成したことや努力したことについて3分以上の会話ができるようになる。また200語以上の essay を書けるようになること。
時　間	50分×2（ライティングの下書きとペア・コメント活動を行う場合は50分×4）
準備物	ワークシート，評価表1・2，リスニング活動用の音声や映像，タイマー

1. タスクの進め方

○Pre-task

1. 教師は生徒に2人1組の Speaking test を行うことおよび Essay Writing の連絡をする。Speaking test については，当日までにだれと当たるかはわからないことを伝える。また，Speaking test と Essay Writing の評価基準を伝える。

2. Step1として，サンプルの essay を読ませ，内容に関する質問に答えさせる。同様にペアで答えを確認させてから，全体で確認する。内容確認後，再度黙読させ，ペアで意見交換させる。

○Task

1. Step2として，自分の目標・挑戦および課題・努力についてブレーンストーミングをさせ，できる限り多くの考えを書かせる。

2. Speaking test の Model Dialog を教師とボランティアの生徒でやってみせる。

3. Step3として，Speaking test の練習を兼ねて，Timed-Conversation をさせる。何も見ずに話せるようにするため，1回目はワークシートを見て，2回目はワークシートをなるべく見ずに，3回目以降はワークシートを見ずに会話活動を行うように指示を出す。
　　会話が終わった後で，ワークシートにペアとの会話内容についてメモをさせる。

○Additional Task

（Personal Statement の Essay Writing を授業内で行う場合の手順例）

4. Step4として，Step1で扱った Personal Statement の例を見せて，First Draft を書き始めるように指示する。

5. Step5として，First Draft をペアで交換させ，内容に関して質問およびコメントを書かせる（3回が望ましい）。

6. Step6として，ペアからの質問やコメントを基に Second Draft を書く。

7. Step7として，Second Draft をペアで交換させ，内容に関して質問およびコメントを書かせる（3回が望ましい）。

8. Step8として，ペアからの質問やコメントを基に Final Essay を書かせる。

2. ワンポイント・アドバイス

・Listening 活動のための音声およびモデルの Speaking test は，ALT との会話をあらかじめ録画（または録音）しておく。

・Authenticity を高めるためにボランティアの生徒2名に協力してもらうとより好ましい。

・コミュニケーション英語もしくは英語論理表現で似たような題材を扱う場合は，その科目の担当の先生と打ち合わせることで反復活動になるため効果的になる。

（柴田直哉）

Work Sheet

My endeavor and accomplishment
自分が達成したことや努力したこと

Goals : (1) You will be able to have three-minute English conversations about your endeavor and accomplishments.

(2) You will be able to write a 200-word personal statement about your endeavor and accomplishments.

Step1 〈Reading〉 Read the sample personal statement and answer the following four comprehension questions.

Personal Statement: My endeavor and accomplishment

I have been playing tennis since I was in primary school. Although I sometimes want to give up playing tennis when I lose games, I always decide to continue to improve my tennis skills. As a result, I have the power of perseverance to make achievements. For example, last year, I was chosen as a member of an international tennis team. At that time, I really wanted to join the international tennis tournament, so I did two main activities to achieve this goal: running and press-ups.

As I lacked physical strength, I decided to run 5 km every morning and every night with my father. I did it for six months until my coach announced the regular members of an international tennis team. It was challenging to keep running at first, so I walked when I had difficulty breathing. However, as I continued the routine, I realized my appropriate running pace. I also gradually became able to run a longer distance without a problem. This endeavor enabled me to play tennis in good physical condition.

In addition to running every day, I also did 200 press-ups before taking a bath every night because press-ups are great exercises to train inner muscles. Similar to when I started to run 5 km, I could not do 200 press-ups easily at first. Although I sometimes wanted to decrease the number of times, I always kept the routine the same. As a result, I was able to do 200 press-ups. I also had a good posture when I joined an international tennis tournament.

Running and press-ups might be considered basic exercises. However, doing these activities for a long time developed my physical and mental strengths. Both jogging and press-ups improved my power of perseverance. More importantly, the power of perseverance is always essential to continue to endeavor and make an accomplishment. Therefore, without running 5 km and doing 200 press-ups for half a year, I would not be able to become a member of an international tennis team.

Q1. What was the author's accomplishment?

＿＿＿＿＿＿＿＿＿＿＿＿＿＿＿＿＿＿＿＿＿＿＿＿＿＿＿＿＿＿＿＿＿＿＿＿

Q2. What did the author do to make an achievement?

＿＿＿＿＿＿＿＿＿＿＿＿＿＿＿＿＿＿＿＿＿＿＿＿＿＿＿＿＿＿＿＿＿＿＿＿

Q3. Why did the author choose to do these activities in order to accomplish his or her goal?

＿＿＿＿＿＿＿＿＿＿＿＿＿＿＿＿＿＿＿＿＿＿＿＿＿＿＿＿＿＿＿＿＿＿＿＿

Q4. What does the author think is necessary to endeavor to be successful?

＿＿＿＿＿＿＿＿＿＿＿＿＿＿＿＿＿＿＿＿＿＿＿＿＿＿＿＿＿＿＿＿＿＿＿＿

Step2 〈Brainstorming/Mind mapping〉 Brainstorm your endeavor and accomplishment. There are sample clue questions below.

Q : What is your biggest achievement?

Q : What did you do to make the accomplishment?

Q : How long did you do these activities until you achieved it?

★ Now, write as many ideas as possible below.

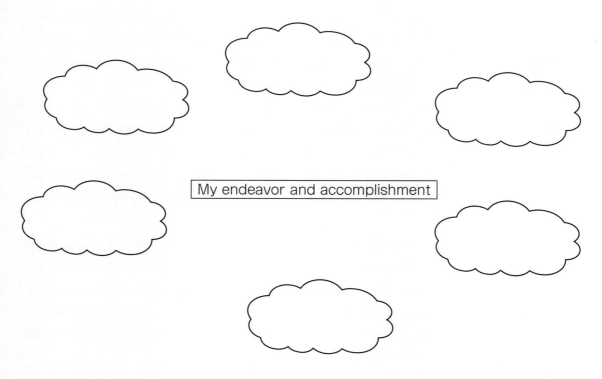

My endeavor and accomplishment

Step3 〈Timed-Conversation〉 "My endeavor and accomplishment" is your essay topic. This activity is useful for you to complete your personal statement. There are four sample questions below. You will need to use as many conversational strategies as possible to keep a conversation with your partner.

★ First-trial : 2 minutes　　Second-trial : 2.5 minutes　　Last-trial : 3 minutes

〈The list of conversation strategies〉
opener / How about you? / shadowing / rejoinders / follow up questions / closer
Could you say that again, please? ← Use this, if you don't understand what your partner says.

(1)　What is your biggest accomplishment?

_____

_____

(2)　What did you do to make the achievement?

_____

_____

(3)　How long did you do the activity until you made the accomplishment?

_____

_____

(4)　What else did you do to accomplish it?

_____

_____

★ Memo for Timed-Conversation : Please write about your partner's story below.

Name	Accomplishments	Effort(s)	The Lengths of the Endeavors

⟨Model Dialog⟩

A : Hi, (Name)‼

B : Oh, hello, (Name)‼ How's it going?

A : I'm good. How about you? You look a little bit stressed.

B : Yeah, I am a little bit frustrated.

A : Oh, why? What's wrong?

B : I need to write a personal statement for my future career, but I don't come up with any ideas to write about.

A : Ah, I see. Maybe you can write about your effort and achievement. Let me ask you some questions. Is that okay?

B : Absolutely‼ It would be a great help to me!

A : Cool. Okay, so what is your biggest achievement?

B : Hmmm …. I'm not sure if this is my biggest achievement, but I was chosen as an international tennis team member last year.

A : Right‼ I remember you joined an international tennis tournament! It was definitely one of your greatest accomplishments‼ Okay, what did you do to make the achievement?

B : Ahhhh … I tried to work out so hard every day!

A : Yeah, I think you did, but how?

B : Actually, I did many things. For example, I ran 5 km every morning and every night with my father. I also did 200 press-ups every day!

A : What!? 5 km every morning and every night!? Did you run before and after class every day!?

B : Hahaha, yeah, I ran 10 km in total every day! I really wanted to be a member of the international tennis team!

A : How long did you do it until your coach selected you as a team member?

B : Oh, this is a great question. I did it for about half a year.

A : Wow‼ That's why you never lost any games in the tournament‼ You should write about it in your personal statement‼

B : Okay‼ Thank you very much for your advice‼ I have some ideas about my personal statement now!

【評価表 1：Rubric for Speaking test】

Speaking Topic：My endeavor and accomplishment

Description：・3分間あなたの努力や達成したことについて話してください。

・例や経験や理由を含めて自分の考えを述べてください。

・できる限り多くの Conversational strategies および Follow-up questions を用いてください。

Categories	Criteria & Points		
	A	B	C
(1) Fluency	3分間会話が不自然に止まることなく，とても流暢に続いた。(7 points)	不自然に止まることが度々あったが，3分間会話がほとんど流暢に続いた。(4 points)	不自然に止まることが多かったが，3分間会話が何とか続けられた。(1 point)
(2) Clarity of Content	例や理由がとても明確で筋道が通っていた。(5 points)	例や理由に不明瞭な点が少しあるが，筋道が通っていた。(3 points)	例や理由に不明瞭な点が多く，あまり明確ではなかった。(1 point)
(3) Target Grammar	過去時制の規則変化・不規則変化を共に正確に使えており，意思疎通ができていた。(5 points)	過去時制の規則変化・不規則変化使用の誤用がわずかにあったが，ほとんど正確に使えており，意思疎通ができていた。(3 points)	過去時制の規則変化・不規則変化の誤用が目立っていたが，意思疎通には問題がなかった。(1 point)
(4) Strategies	Conversation-strategies および Follow-up questions を常に適切な時に用いて，相手に意見や考えを述べる機会をうまく与えられた。(8 points)	Conversation-strategies および Follow-up questions を大抵適切な時に用いることができたが，相手に意見や考えを述べる機会をあまりうまく与えられていなかった。(5 points)	Conversation-strategies および Follow-up questions を用いることがあまりできておらず，一方的に話しがちだった。(2 points)

／25

【評価表２：Rubric for Essay Writing】

Essay Topic：My endeavour and accomplishment

Description：・200語以上で自分の努力と達成についてパーソナルステートメントを書いてください。

・イントロダクション・ボディ・コンクルージョンに分け，最低でも４段落書いてください。

・エッセイの最後に語数を必ず書いてください。

Categories	Criteria & Points		
	A	B	C
(1) **Length**	200語以上 （6 points）	150〜199語 （4 points）	100〜149語 （2 point）
(2) **Clarity of Content**	各段落において主張・例等がとても明確に書かれており，説得力がかなりある。 （8 points）	各段落において主張・例等が明確に書かれており，やや説得力がある。 （5 points）	各段落において主張・例等が不明瞭であり，説得力があまりない。 （2 points）
(3) **Paragraph Construction**	Introduction, Body, Conclusion がとても明確である。また各段落のトピックセンテンス・サポート・結論が明確に書かれており，よく構成されている。 （8 points）	Introduction, Body, Conclusion がある。各段落においてトピックセンテンス・サポート・結論が書かれている。 （5 points）	Introduction, Body, Conclusion が不明瞭である。また，各段落においてトピックセンテンス・サポート・結論がきちんと書かれていない。 （2 points）
(4) **Target Grammar**	過去時制の規則変化・不規則変化を共に正確に使えている。 （5 points）	過去時制の規則変化・不規則変化をやや正確に使えている。 （3 points）	過去時制の規則変化・不規則変化をあまり正確に使えていない。 （1 point）
(5) **Communicability**	意味・内容理解を妨げる文法ミスがとても少ないため，内容が理解しやすい。 （3 points）	意味・内容理解を妨げる文法ミスが少しあるが，内容を理解できる。 （2 points）	意味・内容理解を妨げる文法ミスが多くあるが，かろうじて内容を理解できる。 （1 point）

／30

Task15　My future goals and dreams（Review）
すべての文法事項　最後のパフォーマンス・テストに向けて

目標	将来の夢や目標について，Communication Strategies を適切に使用しながら，3分間，クラスメートと話すことができるようになる。
時間	50分×2（2コマ）
準備物	ワークシート，評価表1・2，タイマー，カラーのペン等

1.　タスクの進め方

○Pre-task

1. 次のパフォーマンステストの概要を伝える。Speaking test と Essay Writing の評価基準を発表する。

2. Step1として，ALT（または生徒一人）と，Model Dialog を読みながら紹介する。英語で Model Dialog を参考に話し終えた後，ポイントとなる部分を必要に応じて日本語で確認する。

3. Step2として，Mind Map を作成させる。文章でなく，キーワードで記入することを確認し，思いついたことをどんどん書いていくように指導する。

4. Step3として，4つの質問に対して自分の答えを書かせる。

5. Step4として，オリジナルの質問を作成させる。質問が完成したら，それぞれに自分の答えを書かせる。

○Task

1. Step5として，Speaking test の練習をペアで行う。ペアを変えて数回行う。1回ごとに，ペアで会話が終わったら，内容について表に記入させる。3回目からは，Model Dialog を見ないで会話をさせる。その際，Step3にある質問だけでなく，Step4で作成したオリジナルの質問や会話の流れに沿った即興の質問にもチャレンジするよう促す。

2. Step6として，Essay Writing（宿題）の説明をする。思いつくままに書くのではなく，構成を考えさせる（メモを作成）。次回の授業で，2名ずつ Speaking test を受ける際，待っている生徒は Essay Writing を書き始める。評価基準を踏まえて essay を書くように指示をする。

2.　ワンポイント・アドバイス

・Mind Map でペンが進まない生徒が多い場合は Step2までやった後に，ペアを変えて，Mind Map をお互いに見せながら，3つずつ質問する時間を設ける。相手に聞かれたことから，アイデアを得て，考えを膨らませることができる。　　　　　　　（竹内愛子）

Work Sheet

My future goals and dreams
最後のパフォーマンス・テストに向けて

今回のパフォーマンステストでは，皆さんの将来の夢や目標について，語ってもらいます。

■トピック：高校卒業後にやりたいこと，目標，夢

■形式と内容：クラスメートと1対1の会話形式。これまでに習ってきた Communication Strategies を，できるだけ使うこと。（注）カンペなしです！

■時間：2人で3分

■評価：ルーブリック（評価表）に従い評価します。

Step1 Read the model dialog and instructions in Japanese below. Then, listen to the model dialog between the ALT and the JET.

〈Model Dialog〉

A：Hi, (partner's name).

B：Hi, (partner's name). {Are you ready? / Let's start.}

※時間の関係で，挨拶は短く。

A：Ok, {   ?}

B：{Well, / Let me see.} {I'd like to / My plan・goal (for my future/after the graduation from Midori high school) is _____.}

A：{Wow, great! / Oh, really? etc.} {How interesting! / Sounds interesting! etc.} Could you tell me more about it?

B：{Sure. / Ok.} （いつ）何歳頃_____，（どこで）_____，（何の分野で）_____，（だれのために／だれと共に）_____，（何をするか）_____

やりたいこと、計画、目標

※2，3文程度，具体的に紹介する。

A：{I see. / I understand. / I like your idea, too. etc.}
{How did you know _____? / Why did/do you _____?
When did / will you _____? / Who gave you _____?
Have you ever met _____? / Are you going to _____? etc.}

B：{Well, / Let me see. etc.} （質問に対する答え）_____.

質問

※WH Q や Yes/No Q をいくつか用意しておく（できるだけ重ならないように）。

* Change roles

A：Nice talking with you.

B：You, too.

沈黙のまま時間が来るのを待つという状況は，失格です。時間が来たら，相手が話しているのに打ち切るのではなく，切りのいいところまで話してから，最後の挨拶に進んでください。大人の会話として，「不自然ではない流れ」が大切です！

Class____ No.____ Name_____

Step2 〈Mind Map〉 Make your mind map about the topic. Expand your ideas.

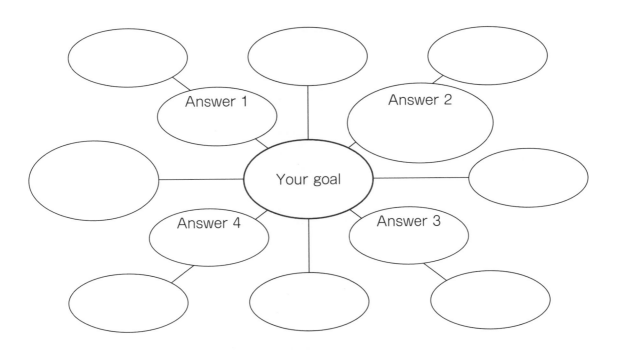

Step3 Questions about this topic

Q1. What's your next goal after graduating from high school?

_____

Q2. When and why did you start to think about it?

_____

Q3. What will you be able to do when you make your goal come true?

_____

Q4. What are you doing now to achieve your goal?

_____

Step4 Make the original questions you want to ask your classmates (2 WH
        questions + 2 Yes/No questions), then write your answer to them.

★ WH question

(1) Q : _____ ?

     A : _____ .

(2) Q : _____ ?

     A : _____ .

★ Yes/No question

(1) Q : _____ ?

     A : _____ .

(2) Q : _____ ?

     A : _____ .

Step5 Practice for the performance test. Based on Step1, 2, and 3, you will
        practice the conversation with your classmates. You can ask your original
        questions above. Also, it is good to ask incidental questions with a good
        flow in the conversation （会話の中で流れに沿ったその時に思いついた質問◎）.
        Make sure to use the conversation strategies you have learned. Before
        starting, check the rubric to ensure improvement in your speaking skills.
        (See the Evaluation form 1).

〈Memo〉 質問や回答で，言いたかったのにうまく言えなかったこと，うまく言えて本番でも
       言いたいことなどを，メモしましょう。

Partner's Name	Questions	Answers

Step6 Essay Writing (homework!)

Look at your mind map and review QA section again and think about the structure of your English essay. Check the rubric before writing.

⟨Structure Notes⟩

· Introduction

· Body 1

· Body 2

· Conclusion

Title : _____

_____

_____

_____

_____

_____

_____

_____

_____

_____

_____

_____

(   ) words

【評価表１：Speaking test】

観点		評価基準	得点
(1) 話し方	**Attitude Delivery**	・話す時は必ずアイコンタクトをして，表情豊かに，コミュニケーションを積極的にとろうという態度で話せた。	2
		・時々，相手の目を見ずに話したり，表情がなかったり，コミュニケーションを積極的にとろうという態度ではなかった。	1
		・ほとんど相手の目を見ずに話したり，表情がなかったり，消極的な態度でコミュニケーションをとっていた。	0
	Pronunciation Voice	・常に英語らしい発音で，大きな声で明瞭に話せた。	2
		・概ね英語の発音のミスなく，聞こえる声で話せた。	1
		・カタカナ発音，日本語の使用，聞き取りにくいところのある話し方だった。	0
(2) 流暢さ	**Skills**	・様々な Fillers や Comments，聞き返しの表現を使うことができた（５種類以上）。	2
		・Fillers や Comments，聞き返しの表現を少し使うことができた（３，４種類）。	1
		・Fillers や Comments，聞き返しの表現をほとんど使うことができなかった（０〜２種類）。	0
	Fluency	・沈黙なく，３分間，流暢に会話を続けることができた。	2
		・５秒くらいの不自然な間は１，２回あったが，ある程度会話を続けることができた。	1
		・５秒くらいの不自然な間が何度もあったり，長い沈黙があったり，会話をあまり続けられなかった（会話をせず，終了のベルが鳴るのを待った）。	0
(3) 内容	**Contents**	・すべての質問や回答が，テーマ（話の流れ）に適切だった。	2
		・質問や回答が，時々，テーマ（話の流れ）からそれることがあった。	1
		・質問や回答が，よくテーマ（話の流れ）からそれた。	0
(4) 正確さ	**Accuracy**	・質問も回答も，概ね正確に伝えることができた。	2
		・（文法・語彙に）時々，間違いがあったが，伝えることができた。	1
		・（文法・語彙に）よく間違いがあり，正確に伝えることができなかった。	0

／12

Class____ No.____ Name_____

【評価表2：Essay Writing】

観点		評価基準	得点
(1) 量	Length	・100語以上書いている。	4
		・81〜99語書いている。	3
		・61〜80語書いている。	2
		・60語以下である。	1
(2) 構成	Structure	・適切な4段落構成で，段落同士のつながりもよい。ディスコースマーカーを適切に3回以上使用している。	4
		・4段落構成で書いているが，段落同士のつながりがよくない。または，ディスコースマーカーを3回以上使用しているが，誤った使用が含まれる。	3
		・4段落構成で書いていない。または，ディスコースマーカーの使用が2回。	2
		・4段落構成で書いていない。または，ディスコースマーカーの使用が1回以下。	1
(3) 内容	Contents	・オリジナリティのある内容で，具体的に，読者にわかりやすく書いている。高校卒業後にやりたいこと／それを考えるようになったきっかけ／それが実現するとどうなるか／それを実現するために今努力していること，すべてに言及している。	4
		・具体的に書いているが，オリジナリティがやや弱い。または，高校卒業後にやりたいこと／それを考えるようになったきっかけ／それが実現するとどうなるか／それを実現するために今努力していることのうち3つしか言及していない。	3
		・オリジナリティのある内容だが，具体性に欠ける。または，高校卒業後にやりたいこと／それを考えるようになったきっかけ／それが実現するとどうなるか／それを実現するために今努力していることのうち2つしか言及していない。または，同じことをくり返し書いている。	2
		・オリジナリティも，具体性も欠ける。または，高校卒業後にやりたいこと／それを考えるようになったきっかけ／それが実現するとどうなるか／それを実現するために今努力していることのうち1つしか言及していない。	1
(4) 正確さ	Accuracy	・適切な文法，語彙，つづり，符号を用いて書いている。誤りなし。	4
		・誤り1，2つ。	3
		・誤り3，4つ。	2
		・誤り5つ以上。	1

／16

Task16

Full debate（Review）
すべての文法事項　反ばくを用いたディベートに挑戦！

目　標	Full debate（反ばくを用いる）に挑戦する。
時　間	50分×2
準備物	ワークシート，評価表

1．タスクの進め方

○Pre-task

1．Step1：教師がトピック（例：cell phones）を導入して，proposition（提案：School children should be allowed to have cell phones.）を示す。宿題として，生徒に affirmative（pro）と negative（con）サイドそれぞれの argument と support を調べさせて書かせておく。support については source を明記させる。

2．Step2：生徒をペアにして，pro，con の argument をそれぞれ紹介する。

○Task

1．Step3：生徒をペアにして，pro，con のサイドをじゃんけんで決めさせて，debate の練習をする。Model Dialog にしたがって，pro サイドが argument を言う。con サイドが要約する。その後，refutation（反ばく）をさせる。refutation をする際は，"It is easy to solve" などを使わせる。最後に，con サイドの argument を言う。同様に pro サイドが，要約，反ばくをする。ペアを変えて，3，4回くり返す。

2．4人グループを作る。じゃんけんで2ペアに分かれる。それぞれのペアの代表がじゃんけんをして，サイドを決める。ペアで話し合いをさせて，argument を2つ選ばせる。それぞれのペアで，順番（例：Pro 1, Pro 2）を決めさせる。

3．Step4：Model Dialog にしたがって，2 on 2で Full debate を教室の前でやらせる。Pro 1と Con 2の生徒は，conclusion を言わせる（例：We gave two strong arguments, so we will win this debate.）。他の生徒は，どちらのチームが勝ったのか評価をする。

2．ワンポイント・アドバイス

・宿題として，事前に賛成，反対の両方の理由を調べさせるとよい。両方のサイドの準備をさせておく。support の source については，生徒のレベルによっては，英語のサイドを使わせるとよい。4人グループおよびサイドは，Full debate の当日に決める。

・時間があれば，debate の後，Essay Writing までさせるとよい。

（佐藤一嘉）

Class____ No.____ Name_____

Work Sheet

Full debate
反ばくを用いたディベートに挑戦！

Step1 Homework（"Get Ready"）

Step2 With your partner, share your pro and con arguments.

Step3 Choose your side (affirmative, negative) in pairs and practice a debate (Pro side starts!).

Resolution : School children should be allowed to have cell phones.

〈Model Dialog〉

A : How are you doing?

B : I'm Ok. How about you?

A : I'm pretty good. Do you agree that school children should be allowed to have cell phones.

B : Yes, I do. Because parents can contact their children in case of an emergency. According to the Asahi Shimbun ….

A : <u>Let me summarize what you said.</u> You agree that … because …. I see your point, but I disagree with you, because it is easy to solve. Instead of a cell phone, children can use a GPS talk. Now I will tell you my con argument. According to the London School of Economics, student performance in exams significantly increased at schools where cell phones were banned.

  <u>Let me summarize what you said.</u> You disagree that … because …. I get your point. But it is not always true, because ….

B : Nice talking with you.

A : You, too.

Step4 Full debate (2 on 2)

Affirmative side (Pros)

1. The first argument

2. Summary, refutation, the second argument

1. Summary, refutation, conclusion

Negative side (Cons)

1. Summary, refutation, the first argument

2. Summary, refutation, the second argument, conclusion

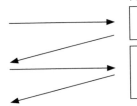

Get Ready : Homework

   Topic 1 : School children should be allowed to have cell phones.

★ PRO : Argument

_____

_____

〈Support / Statistics〉

_____

_____

_____

_____

_____

_____

〈Source (name of website is preferred over address)〉

_____

_____

★ CON : Argument

_____

_____

〈Support / Statistics〉

_____

_____

_____

_____

_____

〈Source (name of website is preferred over address)〉

_____

_____

Class＿＿＿ No.＿＿＿ Name＿＿＿＿＿＿＿＿＿＿＿＿＿＿＿＿

【評価表：Rubric for Debate test】

Categories	Criteria & Points
(1) **Arguments / Supports**	5　Clear arguments for pro/con with good support and with very accurate grammar 3　With only a few grammatical mistakes 1　Not clear arguments for pro/con … with several grammatical mistakes
(2) **Refutation**	5　Good refutation with good support and with very accurate grammar 3　With only a few grammatical mistakes 1　Not clear refutation … with several grammatical mistakes
(3) **Summary &** **Discussion Strategies**	5　Good summary and use of conversation and discussion strategies 3　Appropriate summary and some use of conversation and discussion strategies 1　Not clear summary and less use of conversation and discussion strategies
(4) **Delivery** Pronunciation / Intelligibility 　・Is intelligible 　・Intonation is generally appropriate 　・Sentence and word stress is generally accurately placed Volume 　・Can be clearly heard Fluency 　・Produces extended stretches of language despite some hesitation Eye contact 　・Maintains comfortable eye contact	5　Good pronunciation, volume, fluency, and eye contact 3　Appropriate pronunciation, volume, fluency, and eye contact 1　Not appropriate pronunciation, volume, fluency, and eye contact

／20

【執筆者紹介】

奥田紀子　　愛知県公立高校教諭
　　　　　　名古屋外国語大学大学院 TESOL プログラム（修士）修了
佐藤一嘉　　名古屋外国語大学教授
猿渡由果　　愛知県公立高校教諭
　　　　　　名古屋外国語大学大学院 TESOL プログラム（修士）修了
　　　　　　ハワイ・パシフィック大学大学院 TESOL プログラム（MA）修了
柴田直哉　　名古屋外国語大学言語教育開発センター講師
　　　　　　名古屋外国語大学大学院 TESOL プログラム（修士）修了
竹内愛子　　名古屋市立高校教諭
　　　　　　名古屋外国語大学大学院 TESOL プログラム（修士）修了
　　　　　　ハワイ・パシフィック大学大学院 TESOL プログラム（MA）修了
藤本貴之　　愛知県公立高校教諭
　　　　　　名古屋外国語大学大学院 TESOL プログラム（修士）修了
Yoshi ゼミ　名古屋外国語大学佐藤一嘉英語教育研究ゼミナールの学生
　　　　　　卒業生の多くは英語教師として活躍している。

【編著者紹介】

佐藤　一嘉（さとう　かずよし）

オーストラリア，クイーンズランド大学にて，MA および Ph. D.（応用言語学）を取得。名古屋外国語大学英米語学科英語教育専攻教授。同大学院 TESOL（英語教授法）コース主任。専門分野は，第 2 言語習得研究，外国語教授法，教師教育。
著書は，『英語教育選書　理論と実践でわかるフォーカス・オン・フォーム&パフォーマンス・テスト再入門』（明治図書，2022），『授業をグーンと楽しくする英語教材シリーズ　フォーカス・オン・フォームを取り入れた英文法指導ワーク&パフォーマンス・テスト』（中学 1 年〜中学 3 年，編著，明治図書，2019），『授業をグーンと楽しくする英語教材シリーズ　ワーク&評価表ですぐに使える！英語授業を変えるパフォーマンス・テスト』（全 4 巻，編著，明治図書，2014），『授業をグーンと楽しくする英語教材シリーズ　フォーカス・オン・フォームでできる！　新しい英文法指導アイデアワーク』（全 4 巻，編著，明治図書，2012），"Communities of Supportive Professionals"（共編著，TESOL，2005）など。
論文は，"Longitudinal research on EFL teacher professional development in (Japanese) contexts: Collaborative action research projects"（共著，Language Teaching Research，2022），"Communicative language teaching (CLT) : Practical understandings"（共著，Modern Language Journal，1999）など多数。
「アクション・リサーチから学ぶ英語教授法」（ジャパンライム社）の授業ビデオシリーズ監修。

授業をグーンと楽しくする英語教材シリーズ48

フォーカス・オン・フォームを取り入れた
英文法指導ワーク&パフォーマンス・テスト　高校

2024年5月初版第1刷刊　Ⓒ編著者　佐　藤　一　嘉
　　　　　　　　　　発行者　藤　原　光　政
　　　　　　　　　　発行所　明治図書出版株式会社
　　　　　　　　　　　　　　http://www.meijitosho.co.jp
　　　　　　　　　　(企画)木山麻衣子　(校正)有海有理
　〒114-0023　東京都北区滝野川7-46-1
　振替00160-5-151318　電話03(5907)6702
　　　　　　　　　ご注文窓口　電話03(5907)6668

＊検印省略　　　　組版所　藤　原　印　刷　株　式　会　社

Printed in Japan　　　　　ISBN978-4-18-263825-1
もれなくクーポンがもらえる！読者アンケートはこちらから →